# What if?

## A JOURNEY OF SEEKING, FINDING, AND FOLLOWING

Clare —
I pray that this book
truly blesses you. I'm
so glad our boys sweet
friendship brought us
together! ♡—

**KIM CAMPBELL**

Matthew 6:33

**WHAT IF?**
**A Journey of Seeking, Finding, and Following**
**By Kim Campbell**

Copyright © 2018 Kim Campbell

ISBN: 978-0-692-09911-7

In certain cases, names were changed to protect privacy.

Edited by Lauren Stinton
Cover Design by David Stoddard
Layout by Jonathan McGraw

**www.acresoflove.org**

# DEDICATION

• • •

This book is dedicated to my husband, Mark. You are my best everything. Your love and support have carried me for over twenty years. Thank you for always believing in me and championing me.

This book is also dedicated to my children: Katelyn, Taylor, Avery, and Melo. You are God's greatest gift to me and it's an honor and a privilege to be your mom. Each of you brings me joy beyond measure and I love you . . . too much!

To my sweet friend Gretchen Smith. God brought you into my life at just the right time, and you have been my biggest cheerleader ever since. Thank you for loving me so well.

And finally, to my dearest sister in Christ, Sue Levy. You are the peanut butter to my jelly, my wise council, and my adventure buddy. I love saying, "YES!" to God with you.

# CONTENTS

## PART 4: THE SEARCH FOR MORE OF GOD

# A NOTE FROM GERDA

...

Kim's passion for Jesus is contagious. She doesn't just talk about loving Him—she lives out her faith in small and big ways each day, showing that she is a true follower of Christ.

When I first met Kim, it was in the context of caring for children orphaned in South Africa, and it was an honor to see the transformation in her life as she became an auntie, advocate, and invested emissary for Acres of Love. Her passion to ignite others with her heart for the poor has literally changed her community.

*If anyone builds on this foundation using gold, silver, costly stones, wood, hay or straw, their work will be shown for what it is, because the Day will bring it to light. It will be revealed with fire, and the fire will test the quality of each person's work. If what has been built survives, the builder will receive a reward. - 1 Corinthians 3:12–14 (NIV)*

Gerda Audagnotti
**FOUNDER AND CEO, ACRES OF LOVE**

# INTRODUCTION

...

I was back in South Africa. This was my ninth time visiting the once-orphaned children at Acres of Love. That morning I was enjoying a cup of very strong African coffee at the Vida e Caffe in the Johannesburg airport. Gerda Audagnotti, the founder and CEO of Acres of Love, sat across from me, along with her grown son and two of my closest friends. We were waiting to board our flight to Cape Town.

My friends and I listened in awe, as always, as Gerda told story after story of the miraculous things that had happened in and through Acres of Love. We'd heard about supernatural visitations, financial provision, and miraculous healings, but on this occasion, she was telling us about a little boy named Bongi.

Bongi came to Acres of Love in 1999 as an infant. HIV positive, he was on the brink of death, and Gerda and her team were told he would not survive. They took him in, bathed him, held him, loved him, and prayed for him. But only one day into their care, they realized how sick he was and decided it would be best to move him to a facility called Cotlands, which was a sanctuary for the sickest abandoned babies. The staff from Acres of Love would go visit him there every day, holding him close and praying for him.

Lizzie, one of the volunteers at Cotlands, observed that the babies all around Bongi were dying, but it seemed like Bongi was waiting for his daily visits. She told Gerda, "I know what you do with babies at Acres of Love. I've seen you do it with Bongi. You lay hands on them and you say, 'In Jesus' name,' and you pray for them." Lizzie wasn't a believer in Jesus and didn't understand what all of that meant, but she started praying for Bongi the way she had seen the Acres of Love staff pray for him.

And he lived. Three weeks later, they were able to take him back to Acres of Love, where he continued to get stronger and healthier. He blossomed and grew—a lot—and when he was tested again, he was HIV negative. He was later adopted and is now living with a wonderful family in Sweden.

Our mouths dropped open. Chills raced up our arms, and we sat there shaking our heads in disbelief. Did we just hear her right? Did she just say that God healed a little boy who was dying of AIDS? It was a miracle. This was the most incredible thing I'd ever heard, and questions started running through my head. Why didn't more people know about this? There we were, sitting in the middle of a bustling airport in Africa with so many people coming and going in every direction. But they had no idea what was happening at our table—that our lives were being rocked and that everything was about to change for us. Did they know God heals people? Did they understand that He works miracles today? Everyone needed to know this, because this changed everything.

I leaned forward. "Have you ever thought about documenting the hundreds of amazing stories you've shared with us over the years?" I asked Gerda, knowing it was important for others to have the opportunity to hear what God was doing in and through Acres of Love.

She said she'd considered it, but she was so busy doing the work that she couldn't find the time to write all of the stories down. I offered to document the stories for her, and right there in the Johannesburg airport, my vision for this book was born.

When Gerda told me of the miraculous things God was doing in the lives of orphans in South Africa, something happened in my heart. I wanted to know *that* God. I wanted to see the miracles for myself; I wanted to have the encounters, see His face, know His ways, and display His glory. I began a quest to discover what would happen if I put into practice all the things I was learning about Him. I became fascinated with asking, "What if?" What if I acted, on a daily basis, like I really believed what I said I believed? What would my life look like then? As I got the smallest taste of God and began to live a more and more surrendered lifestyle, my heart shifted again, and I started to long for Him with everything in me.

And so, in this book I will share wild, crazy stories of God moving in South Africa, as well as my own personal stories, thoughts, and the revelations He's given me along the way. My intention is to convey truths I have learned and show you the progression of my faith walk—from where I started to how God led me, transformed me, and began to use me. This book is an honest display of my raw relationship with the Lord. I aim to be transparent and vulnerable in order to show what it really looked like in the process.

My ultimate prayer for this book is that it calls you into a deeper relationship with the Lord. It is my goal to ignite a fire inside of you that burns for more of Him. Though I don't consider myself an expert in healing, transformation, and caring for the abandoned and broken, I hope my experiences will spark questions and curiosities within you and send you to the Scriptures, where you can find the truth for yourself.

See this book as an invitation. God is forever inviting us to press in for more of Him.

# Part One

## HOW MY STORY BEGAN

...

# One

## FOXHOLE CHRISTIAN

...

At the end of August 2005, I delivered my second daughter, Taylor, and something went wrong. While administering my epidural, the anesthesiologist gave me a "wet tap." This is an accidental puncture of the dura, which is the tough outermost membrane enveloping the spinal cord. When this happens, spinal fluid begins to leak out of the tiny hole. The brain floats in this fluid, so as the liquid slowly leaks, the brain tends to sag, straining the connective tissues and causing a horrific spinal headache.

Debilitating head pain set in. My fever steadily increased and finally reached 105 degrees. The doctors and nurses couldn't understand why there was a fever at all because it wasn't typical of a wet tap, and they began to worry about some sort of infection. So they cleared the room and took Taylor away from me, sending her down to the nursery. I hated being separated from my newborn baby girl, but I was so sick and in so much pain that I couldn't even hold her. All the doctors and nurses would put on gowns, masks, and gloves before entering my hospital room. They put a caution sign on my door that warned everyone I was in quarantine, and they took full measures to prevent the spread of any infection to the rest of the labor and delivery unit.

Late that afternoon, the sun began beating into my hospital room. At the moment, no one else was there with me. My husband, Mark, had gone home for a few hours to spend time with our twenty-one-month-old daughter, Katelyn. The pain was horrible, and in my delirium, my fear was through the roof. I was practically in a panic, certain that they weren't going to figure out what was wrong with me.

*I'm going to die,* I thought, convinced. *How could this be happening? Where did this all go wrong? I came in here a healthy young woman and delivered a perfect baby girl, and now all hell is breaking loose. What is Mark going to do if I die? I am going to leave him all alone to raise two little girls. He is going to be devastated. This will crush him. What about my daughters? They will never even know me. I am going to miss everything.*

With my eyes squinted and my head pounding, I crawled onto my knees. I was a mess; my blue hospital gown was falling off my shoulder and draped down to expose my chest. I pushed my matted hair out of my sweaty face, folded my trembling hands together, and through uncontrollable tears, I prayed. I had probably prayed only a handful of times in my life, and it had been at least ten years since the thought had even crossed my mind. My parents weren't believers. I'd spent a couple of years in middle school going to Sunday school and church camp with friends, but I didn't really believe in God. In fact, I was often outspoken to the point of being disrespectful about how religion was a crutch for weak people, and I'd done my fair share of dabbling in New Age practices and Buddhism. However, on that scary afternoon, I was vulnerable and desperate and willing to try anything.

"God? Please, please, please . . . I don't want to die. I'm begging You—don't let me die. I'll do anything. I promise, if You let me live, I will figure this whole thing out. I will search for You. Please!" I collapsed into a pile on the bed and just wept. Like a soldier in battle,

I cried out from inside my foxhole and made a desperate final plea for mercy.

A team of nurses rushed in, stripped me out of my hospital gown and frantically ran around getting washcloths that they soaked in a bucket of ice water and put all over my body. They brought in a huge high-powered fan and set it up to blow directly on me. And worse, they put a frozen blanket underneath me. It was painfully cold but critical to bring down my dangerously high fever. By this time, Mark was back and my parents were also there. My mom kept an icy cold washcloth on my forehead and ran her fingers through my hair. My dad kept sweetly attempting to rub my back, as he always did when I was sick, but it hurt too much.

Before long, an infectious disease doctor came in and introduced himself to us. He'd accidentally stepped out of the elevator onto the labor and delivery floor, and one of the nurses asked him to take a quick look at me. Confused by my symptoms, he ordered a series of tests, including a spinal tap, and immediately got me started on a heavy cocktail of antibiotics. By the next morning, I was feeling better and the fever was down. They allowed Taylor back into my room, and my heart just melted as I held her and was able to nurse her again. Mark went home to pick up Katelyn, and there in the hospital, we got to be a family again; it was nearly overwhelming to have my two girls and my husband with me. Happy to be alive, I just wanted to go home, so all of us could begin our life together.

A couple of days later, they inserted a PICC line into my arm and trained Mark on how to administer antibiotics through the IV, which he would need to do several times throughout the day for the next two weeks. Then they sent us home. When we later saw the infectious disease doctor at his private practice, he told me I had contracted bacterial meningitis from the wet tap.

This whole experience was terrifying. I realized how powerless I really was, how little control I had over my life; I was literally brought to my knees and forced to admit that I was *not* in control. For the first time, I recognized my need for God and called out to Him for help. I was so grateful that He heard me and rescued me, and I wanted to hold up my end of the bargain.

I was going to discover who He really was.

# Two

## BIBLE BANGER

...

A few months passed before I remembered the deal I'd made with God from my hospital bed. Somewhat reluctantly, I began to do research and ended up spending hours on the computer looking at websites of all the churches in my city, trying to find a place that mentioned God but didn't seem too focused on this whole "Jesus Christ" thing. That name, for whatever reason, really irritated me and sparked a series of uncomfortable feelings. I wondered what the big deal was with this Jesus guy. Why was everyone so committed to including Him on all the church websites? Who was He, anyway?

One Sunday in November, I attended San Clemente Presbyterian Church because I'd heard a lot of good stuff about it from people in my neighborhood. I sat in the back on the aisle, so I could sneak out at any point during the service. As I looked around, I checked out the other attendees and they seemed normal. They were much hipper than I expected church folk to be. I figured everyone would be pretty conservative, wearing pearls and suits, but the trend seemed to lean more toward Hawaiian shirts and flip-flops. I liked that.

The music was actually pretty cool with drums and a guitar, not just some dusty organ. The people seemed genuinely happy to be there, and to my surprise, I really enjoyed what the pastor had to say. So I went back the next week. And the next and the next.

As my church attendance became a regular thing, Mark gently told me, "I'm really happy for you. I'm glad you've found something. Just please don't start nagging at me to go to church with you." He was raised Catholic and had spent many years in church. He was supportive of my journey but didn't feel the need to pursue his faith on a deeper level.

But by February I had convinced him to come with me and check it out, and he actually liked it there too. I sent an email to the head pastor, Tod Bolsinger, and introduced myself, explaining how I was really new to all of this church stuff and didn't know where to begin. I asked if he would be willing to meet with me so I could ask all my questions: "Am I really supposed to believe all this crazy stuff? Some guy Moses really parted the Red Sea? What about the dinosaurs? And tell me more about this Jesus everyone is so excited about."

Pastor Tod invited me to his office, and over a cup of coffee, he graciously answered all my questions. We met a few times, and he talked me through all my doubts and concerns and prayed for me. He even bought me a Bible and suggested I read it, starting with the book of Matthew. He thought it would be a good idea to really try to get to know Jesus. His advice was to read it as if I believed it and see what happened.

So I did, and somewhere along the way—I have no idea exactly when or how it happened—I started to believe. I didn't make a deliberate decision; I didn't just leap into it blindly, but my heart changed. It wasn't an instant occurrence or something I even noticed as it happened, but one day I realized, "Wait . . . I believe this!" On March 19, 2005, I was baptized along with my daughters. I didn't understand everything—in fact, I didn't understand much—but I had faith and it felt like my life was just beginning.

I quickly developed a veracious appetite for anything God related. Devouring every Christian theology book I could get my hands on, I started attending a weekly Bible study and took seriously my commitment to read God's Word every day. When I discovered I really enjoyed contemporary Christian music, I filled my home and car with praise and worship songs and melted every time I heard my kids singing along. Seemingly on their own, my interests shifted away from certain TV shows and gossip magazines, and I started making new friends who shared my passion for Jesus and the Bible.

My life was changing. I didn't sit down one day and make a big decision to stop doing certain things and start doing others. No one from the church told me how to act or behave, what to do and not do, what was "allowed" and what wasn't. Something was just happening inside of me. As my heart changed, my interests and desires changed too. I wanted more and more of the things of God.

As I studied the Bible and came to know Jesus, I took note of what seemed to be important to Him: the people He spent time with and how He interacted with them. I took special interest in the words Jesus Himself said, things like:

- "God blesses those who are poor and humble, who hunger for justice, who are merciful and work for peace" (Matt. 5).

- "Don't store up your treasures here on earth but in heaven" (Matt. 6:19–20).

- "No one can serve two masters. You can't serve God and money" (Matt. 6:24).

- "Give as freely as you have received" (Matt. 10:8).

- "If any of you wants to be my follower, you must give up your own way, take up your cross, and follow me" (Matt. 16:24).

- "Love your neighbor as yourself" (Mark 12:31).

Jesus was wise and direct, His messages simple but profound. From the beginning, it was crystal clear to me that my faith journey had to be about more than just going to church on Sundays and avoiding serious sins. I realized that following Jesus was different than just believing something new. Faith was an action word, so it should make an impact on me; it should actually change me to the extent that I start to live differently.

As I wrestled with the things I was learning, I tried to figure out how to apply them to my life. In the Gospels, Jesus was always inviting people to follow Him, and I began to wonder what that looked like and meant for me personally. I considered myself a disciple, a student of Jesus, but I couldn't literally follow Him around like the guys in the Bible did. I thought, *He's not here in front of me. I don't see Him. I can't touch Him or talk to Him, so how am I supposed to follow Him? How can I know where He is leading me? How does someone like me, an ordinary person with a family and responsibilities, follow Jesus?*

I once heard Francis Chan say that following Jesus is like playing a game of follow the leader. If the leader puts their hand on their head, you put your hand on your head. If they jump up and down on one foot, you jump up and down on one foot. You do what the leader does and say what the leader says. In the same way, if you are following Jesus, you do what He did and say what He said.

I began to ask myself, *What does my Leader do? What does He say? What does He care about? Who does He spend His time with, and what does He spend His time doing?* It made sense to me that I should care about the same people and do the same kinds of things. If I believed in this Jesus, I should act like it. My actions should reflect my belief in Him and my desire to follow Him and serve Him.

# Three

## THE LEAST OF THESE

• • •

As I began to study the Bible, I noticed that three groups of people seemed to come up over and over again. Orphans, widows, and strangers are at the top of God's priority list. These are the weak, the underprivileged, the outcast, the vulnerable, the poor and needy. Scripture repeatedly mentions the importance of caring for this group. James 1:27 is one instance: "Pure and genuine religion in the sight of God the Father means caring for orphans and widows in distress and refusing to let the world corrupt you."

Jesus, it seemed, had high expectations for me because I called myself His follower. I realized He expected me to seek out and engage with this group, to care for their needs, defend them, love them, and rescue them. He Himself spent so much time among these types of people and had compassion on them, being moved to action on their behalf. His heart was for them, and the time and energy He spent with them and on them reflected His concern. His actions were a direct response to His heart.

In Matthew 25:34–46, Jesus talks about sheep and goats. One day when He sits upon His throne to judge the world, He will separate all people into two groups. At His right hand will be the sheep, those who cared for "the least of these," and at His left hand will be the goats, those who didn't.

*Then the King will say to those on his right, "Come, you who are blessed by my Father, inherit the Kingdom prepared for you from the creation of the world. For I was hungry, and you fed me. I was thirsty, and you gave me a drink. I was a stranger, and you invited me into your home. I was naked, and you gave me clothing. I was sick, and you cared for me. I was in prison, and you visited me."*

*Then these righteous ones will reply, "Lord, when did we ever see you hungry and feed you? Or thirsty and give you something to drink? Or a stranger and show you hospitality? Or naked and give you clothing? When did we ever see you sick or in prison and visit you?"*

*And the King will say, "I tell you the truth, when you did it to one of the least of these my brothers and sisters, you were doing it to me!"*

*Then the King will turn to those on the left and say, "Away with you, you cursed ones, into the eternal fire prepared for the devil and his demons. For I was hungry, and you didn't feed me. I was thirsty, and you didn't give me a drink. I was a stranger, and you didn't invite me into your home. I was naked, and you didn't give me clothing. I was sick and in prison, and you didn't visit me."*

*Then they will reply, "Lord, when did we ever see you hungry or thirsty or a stranger or naked or sick or in prison, and not help you?"*

*And he will answer, "I tell you the truth, when you refused to help the least of these my brothers and sisters, you were refusing to help me."*

24

*And they will go away into eternal punishment, but the righteous will go into eternal life.*

God identifies so closely with the poor that He says the way we treat them is how we treat Him. This passage of Scripture is humbling and, honestly, a little scary. In the end when I stand before the Lord Jesus, I want Him to know me as a person who loved Him and cared deeply about the people He identified with. I want my heart to be so aligned with His that I am like Him, caring about the things and the people He cares about.

My point isn't that we should spend our time doing all the "right" things to earn favor with God. What He really desires is the transformation of our hearts as we grow closer to Him in relationship. He wants us to seek Him, know Him, love Him, and be committed to Him—to be so thankful and filled to overflowing with His grace and mercy that our lives are a natural outpouring of His love inside of us. We get to be yielded vessels, His hands and feet, light to the world.

Commitment to God is accompanied by a transformed heart. He is more interested in our relationship with Him than He is about any good work we can perform. But at the same time, if we are truly seeking to know Him and are in relationship with Him, desiring to be more and more like Him, He will begin to break our hearts for the things that break His heart. We will naturally desire to care for the people He cares about, do the things that He would do, and say the things He would say.

When Jesus says, "Follow Me," I like to imagine that He is right here, a few feet in front of me. He looks back, gives me a smile, and motions for me to catch up. He keeps gently inviting me, "Follow Me. Come on. Follow Me."

I slowly and hesitantly take small steps in His direction. He walks on ahead and all I can see is His back, but every so often He'll turn to check on me. He never looks at me with disappointment or frustration, and He always beckons me with a warm smile, encouraging me to keep following Him. "Come on. This way. Don't be afraid."

As a busy wife and stay-at-home mom, I began to really consider this question: What would following Jesus every day look like? Did my to-do list and daily calendar reflect that I was a follower of Jesus? Did my credit card bill support my claim? Was my minivan parked at the places Jesus would visit? Was I treating my body, the temple of the Holy Spirit, accordingly? I asked God to reveal to me any areas in my life that needed to be refined, any things that needed to go or be added. I kept studying the life of Christ and wanted to "take up my cross," like He talked about, and follow Him.

Wanting to get involved with my new church and serve God with my time and talents, I started working with the high school ministry and began co-leading a small group of ninth-grade girls. My co-leader was a young woman named Kelli, who was a recent college graduate. I learned she worked with a nonprofit called Acres of Love that rescued and cared for orphans in South Africa.

*Africa? Orphans?* Kelli told the most incredible stories about these kids on the other side of the world. Filled with passion for the cause, she had even traveled to South Africa a couple of times. I begged her to tell me more stories and show me pictures. It was like I was magnetically drawn to her and anything she had to say about those kids. Something was happening inside of me; my heart was breaking for these kids and compassion rose up within me. I discovered my own passion for an unexpected group of people: orphans in Africa.

Eventually, I realized God was answering my prayers. He had opened a door for me, bringing Kelli into my life at just the right moment. He knew full well what He was doing and where He was leading me. I had asked and He answered. Everything was about to change.

Everything.

# four

## ACRES OF LOVE

...

Through Kelli and the many books I read on the topic, I learned that at the time, more than 6,500 new HIV infections occurred daily worldwide and about 1,000 of these were in South Africa. AIDS and other factors related to poverty had left the country with approximately three million orphans. It was believed that about 575 children became orphans every single day there. Obviously, this had a huge impact on the community, and there was no system big enough or equipped to care for that number of orphans. AIDS was wiping out an entire generation of people. While the elderly were dying of natural causes, the middle-aged, most productive group—the teachers, nurses, domestic workers, business owners—were becoming infected with HIV and dying. They left children in their wake with no one to step in and care for them. Extended family members felt the overwhelming burden of caring for extra children in their already overcrowded shacks, and lack of money and resources forced them to turn kids away.

Children who become orphans are often found beside their mother's dead body, where they've been sitting for days. They're also found locked in outhouses, thrown down long-drop toilets, and disposed of in trash bags. Groups of children huddle together in cardboard boxes in alleys or sleep in abandoned cars; they hide under bridges and live in the park with stray dogs. They are left in overcrowded hospitals or police stations; they are starved, beaten, and sexually abused. Living in total poverty and helplessness, these kids are hungry, uneducated, victimized, and completely neglected. There are countless "child-headed households," which means that if a sibling group is left alone with no adults to care for them, the oldest child becomes the caretaker, protector, and provider. There are stories of children as young as four years old taking care of an even younger baby sibling, killing bugs to feed them.

The statistics, stories, and images I came across completely wrecked me. I had trouble believing these horrible things were happening—all day, every day—and I hadn't even known about it. I began to wrestle with big and hard questions: How was this fair? Where was God in all this suffering? How was it that my daughters, who just happened to be born to my husband and me in Southern California, had the privilege of living in a beautiful home in a safe neighborhood, had a pantry filled with food, received excellent medical care, and were getting a phenomenal education? How was it that millions of children in Africa, by no fault of their own, were alone, scared, cold, hungry, sick, and abused?

I was distraught just at the idea of my two little girls being out in the world alone, wandering the streets, looking for shelter and food, trying to stay safe. I would walk through fire before I let something like that happen to my own kids. This wasn't right. Now that I knew the truth, I couldn't just stick my head in the sand and pretend I didn't. I had to get involved somehow and make a difference in the lives of these innocent, suffering children in South Africa.

In Richard Stearns' book *The Hole in Our Gospel*, he prays, "Lord, break my heart for the things that break yours."[1] As I struggled with these upsetting facts and was haunted by the images I saw, I began to sense that God was going to use my broken heart. I felt a powerful pull toward South Africa and those who had been orphaned there—which wasn't anything I had ever imagined, chosen, or planned on. But I could see how He was leading my heart in order to use me.

I convinced my apprehensive husband to join me in taking Kelli and another young lady who worked with her out to dinner one night. At the restaurant, I asked them to tell us more about the AIDS pandemic in Africa, to share stories of orphaned children, and to educate us on what Acres of Love was all about.

"What could we do to get involved with this work?" I asked. "How could we be helpful?"

They told me the story of a little girl named Thando. She was just seven years old, and they were trying to raise $15,000 so she could have an important series of surgeries. Before coming to Acres of Love, she and her brother, Nkosi, lived with their uncle after their mother passed away. This uncle abused her and she contracted HIV and HPV (human papilloma virus.) She was sick and in terrible pain.

Without hesitation, I volunteered to help. All I had to do was imagine one of my own daughters going through something like this, and I was compelled to do whatever it took to provide this girl with the medical care she needed.

A few days later, I hosted a meeting in my home. Inviting friends and neighbors over to learn about Acres of Love and hear the stories I had heard, I asked them to join me in raising the money for Thando's surgeries. There was a great response, and we committed to holding a fundraiser.

---

1 Richard Stearns, *The Hole in Our Gospel: What Does God Expect of Us?* (Nashville: Thomas Nelson, 2009).

The Acres of Love staff asked me to send some loose-fitting clothes to Thando. Even pants and shorts were painful for her. I collected several items, wrapped them all up, and wrote a card for her.

But when it came time to sign my name at the bottom, I paused. What should I say? She didn't know me or have any idea who I was. Eventually, I told her I was part of a group of women in America who loved her and prayed for her. I signed the card, "Mommies in America." That became the official name of our donor group. We were mommies on the other side of the world who wanted to give these children in Africa the same opportunities that our children had.

Our fundraiser, A Party with a Purpose, was a huge success. We hosted it at a great beachside restaurant, had amazing food, a live jazz band, and wonderful silent auction baskets. We educated our guests on how the South African children were suffering, spoke of the success that Acres of Love was having in rescuing orphans, and invited everyone to help us meet Thando's urgent medical needs. We raised $26,000 that day! We were ecstatic—and exhausted.

I remember wanting the event to be over, so I could rest. But the morning after the fundraiser, I woke up with fresh resolve and an even deeper passion for this cause and organization. I asked Acres of Love about some of their other needs, and they explained that the home Thando lived in, which was called the Bridges Forever Home, had recently lost its funding. They needed a partner to come alongside them with the required $90,000 a year to operate the home. This money went toward the children's direct care and provided them with food, clothing, medical costs, school fees, therapies, extracurricular activities, etc. While Mark and I certainly didn't have that kind of money ourselves, I felt confident we could come up with it through fundraising.

"I'll do it," I told them, accepting financial responsibility. I began to put all my time and energy into finding a way to provide for those ten children.

A short time later, Acres of Love invited me, along with several others, to travel to South Africa to meet Thando and the other kids in the Bridges Forever Home. I would get to experience the culture, witness the poverty firsthand, understand how the organization worked, and become a more educated ambassador to speak on behalf of these kids.

As usual, it was an easy and energetic "Yes!" for me. However, Mark, the part of my heart that keeps me grounded, was a bit apprehensive. He had some important questions and concerns: How were we going to pay for this expensive trip? Who was going to take care of our two young daughters while I was gone and he was working? Was it responsible for me to leave our family and travel so far away to a dangerous country?

We discussed and argued, prayed and researched, then discussed and argued some more. I felt strongly that if God wanted me to go, He would provide the financial means and take care of me, the girls, and the rest of the details. So I sent out a letter to family and friends asking for financial support in paying the $5,000 necessary to make the trip. In response, I received several generous donations. Right around the time I needed to pay for the trip, two anonymous donations came in on the same day, one for $1,000 and one for $1,500. That was the confirmation Mark and I both needed to know that God was going to take care of everything. Feeling encouraged, and like God was blessing this opportunity, we booked my flight and I was on my way.

The day my group and I landed in South Africa, we spent time in Soweto, which is a group of townships southwest of Johannesburg. A *township* is a residential development for non-whites living near or working in white-only communities. Soweto was the scene of violent anti-apartheid rioting in 1976, when a student protest led to a clash with the police. It is the largest purely black urban settlement in South Africa. There is a poorly planned sewage system, no electricity, and limited water sources.

We walked dirt roads, held hands with the numerous children who approached us for the "biscuits" we were handing out, took photographs of the kids with our digital cameras, and had so much fun showing them how beautiful they were in the pictures. We talked to women in their tiny shacks, watched little kids fill up buckets at the local water spigot, and marveled at ladies carrying heavy loads on their heads and others who were going about their business with babies strapped to their backs.

Taking in the sights, sounds, and smells of the area, I wanted to know everything about the large number of kids running around in the streets. They were dirty and barefoot, and they had runny noses and painful-looking rashes. There were no adults in sight; these kids were completely unsupervised. I had so many questions for our group leader: Where did they live? Where were their parents? Did they even have parents? Did they have AIDS? When was the last time they ate? Why weren't they in school? Were they safe? Were they scared? Did they need help?

Acres of Love began the trip this way so we could experience the type of environment out of which many of the children are rescued. It's important to understand what life is like before the kids come to Acres of Love. When donor partners meet the children who have been in the organization's care for a fair amount of time, they don't realize these kids are unrecognizable compared to the way they were on the day they arrived. When they come to Acres of Love, they are often small, underdeveloped, dirty and sick, scared, quiet, showing no emotion, traumatized. But by the time the donor parents meet them, they are gorgeous, clean and beautifully groomed, well rested, and relaxed. Their skin glows, they smile and laugh often, they are confident and friendly, they trust, they play, they are brave enough to act naughty; they know they are safe and secure and loved. But all of this takes time. It is a slow and steady work.

That evening, we returned to our safe and comfortable hotel. Caught in the effects of jet lag, I lay wide awake in the middle of the night for hours, listening to the thunderstorm and trying to process all I had experienced that day. Eventually I got up, turned on the light, and began writing in my journal all the questions that circled through my head: Where were all those children I had been with earlier that day? Did they have shelter from the storm? Were they frightened? Why did I get to enjoy this luxurious hotel room while there were millions of abandoned children out in the storm, and they were sick, scared, wet, and hungry? My heart ached.

I found some peace in knowing that the children rescued by Acres of Love were safe and sound as the storm raged. As I thought about it, I was honored to be a small part of the solution for them and was overwhelmed with thankfulness to God, who had led me to this work, these kids, and this country. Tomorrow I would get to meet Thando and the other kids in the Bridges Forever Home. I had brought all sorts of gifts for them, and the next day on the way to the house, I planned to pick up what we needed to make ice cream sundaes.

At the home, the kids excitedly gave me a tour and proudly showed off their rooms and their beds. We played in the backyard and made giant, delicious sundaes. When they opened their presents, the kids were gracious and grateful. They were beautiful children, well behaved and well adjusted, polite and outgoing, happy and healthy, secure but sweetly attached to their house mom.

It was obvious how much the house mom loved her kids. She was committed to the work and had a passion for it; she spoke of her faith and God's call on her life to be there. Later she told us stories about each of the children, about how they came to Acres of Love and how hard those early years were when they were so sick. She shared what their current health status was, bragged about their individual successes, and confided in us about their trials. She was just like any other mom: invested, proud, concerned, strong, wise, a force to be reckoned with. It was clear the children respected her and that she ran a tight ship. The home was tidy and organized, and everyone took pride in their belongings and family members. They were a close-knit group, respectful of one another and well disciplined. I was impressed.

The unique thing about Acres of Love is their "forever home" model. The homes are in upper middle-class areas and provide the kids with access to good schools, churches, doctors, therapies, and extracurricular activities. The house parents live in the homes with the children and raise them as their very own. This provides a real family feel and removes the revolving door of staff coming in and out on eight-hour shifts. They have consistency and stability, which are so important for children who have endured such trauma.

It was hard to leave the house after only a few hours. I had traveled so far to meet all of them and I wanted to stay longer, but it relieved my heart to see that they were in such good hands. It was clear that they were well taken care of, that Acres of Love was providing them with a wonderful life, and that God had a plan for each of them. I left there with strong confidence in the organization and was proud to be involved in such high-quality work. Now that I knew the kids personally, I was excited to get home and share stories and pictures. I was even more committed to the work that Acres of Love was doing, and I was eager to continue my fundraising efforts on their behalf.

Since that first trip, my relationship with the kids and their house mom has grown stronger and stronger. I've been able to go back and see them at least once a year, and I always send birthday and Christmas gifts and chat with them regularly on WhatsApp. We were even able to fly Nkosi, Thando's brother, out to visit us when he graduated from high school. It's been such an honor to be a part of their lives, and I am grateful for the opportunity to be so personally involved. I truly feel like we are family, like they are my kids on the other side of the world. I have full confidence in the staff members who take care of them, and I am amazed as I watch the children's progress.

Somewhat to my surprise, I found that the hardest part of my first trip to South Africa was returning home. It was in my beautiful beach town, in my safe and friendly neighborhood, in my clean and comfortable two-story home with my healthy family, my full closet, and my stocked refrigerator that I experienced the worst case of culture shock. How was I supposed to return to my lavish and overindulgent lifestyle after all I had just seen? How could I justify buying another new outfit or sitting through another pedicure when I knew that my money literally could be used to save lives?

How would I ever be able to go back to my old way of living?

# five

## NOW WHAT?

•••

Convinced that everything had to change, I decided that the only possible solution was to persuade Mark that we had to sell everything, move to South Africa, and save the children.

As you can imagine, that conversation did not go well. We were out on a date night to reconnect after my trip, and I guess Mark didn't find my wine mixed with a passionately stated, "Let's move to Africa," the most romantic way to spend the evening. We ended up pulling into the parking lot of the local elementary school, me in tears and Mark growing increasingly annoyed. He made it crystal clear that this crazy, far-fetched idea of mine was not going to happen.

"We are not supposed to pack up our lives and move to Africa," he told me. Though he was very supportive of my journey and my commitment to Acres of Love, he didn't feel that moving to Africa was what God was calling our family to do.

Mark and I have always called ourselves a perfect balance. He loves to say that I am the gas and he is the brakes. While I tend to be more emotional and passionate, he is calm, steady, and even keel. As he and I discussed my heart for Africa and what we could do for all those kids, I trusted that God had put us together for a divine reason. Obviously, He wanted to use us as a couple, but we needed to be on the same page.

After a lot of time, prayer, reading, Bible study, and conversations with trusted advisors, I slowly came to agree with Mark and grudgingly put aside the idea to sell everything and move to Africa. But if that wasn't what God had for us, what did He have for us? I really began to seek His plan for my life and the lives of our family. How could I make any tangible, lasting impact on the orphans in South Africa as a wife and mother living in Southern California? How was I supposed to serve Acres of Love when I had errands to run, school conferences to attend, practices to get to, meals to prepare, laundry to fold, noses to wipe, and little ones to tuck in bed? I couldn't make sense of it all and struggled to understand how I could do everything I wanted to as a wife, stay-at-home mom, and passionate orphan advocate.

Slowly God began to speak into my heart. One day I felt like He told me, "You don't have to move to Africa to be used by Me to make an impact. This is your mission field. Serve Me here and you will make a difference over there. Share your life, share your transformation, invite others to join you, and lead them in this work."

Little by little, I realized He wanted me to surrender to Him—to follow Him and be used by Him. Not only did He want me to use my time, talents, and resources to make an impact for Acres of Love, but He wanted to use me right where I was, in the specific location He ordained me to live, with the people He put in my life and the situations I found myself in. He wanted to use me every day, with every person; He had plans for every appointment on my calendar, every dollar I spent, every room of my home, every outfit I put on, every thought I had about my appearance, every thought I posted on social media, every text message I sent, every happy hour where I met my friends, all of my marriage, and all of my time with my children. God wanted all of me.

Acres of Love gave me the title of *emissary;* I would use my voice for the voiceless and plead the cause of these amazing children who were just trying to survive. My Mommies in America group continued to grow and fundraise, and I led trips of women donors to South Africa to meet the children every year. Before I knew it, I had grown a ministry of sorts and was raising up people in my sphere of influence to follow Jesus and care for the "least of these." Women were challenged and transformed, marriages were strengthened, our children were being taught to serve, and our community was becoming more and more informed and passionate about the needs of orphans in South Africa.

# Six

## HE GIVES AND TAKES AWAY

...

I have a vivid memory of sitting on the linoleum floor of the family room in my childhood home. I was watching "60 Minutes" with my Grandpa Charlie, and they were doing a story on how little girls in China were being abandoned. Right then and there, I made the quiet decision in my heart to adopt a little girl from China one day. I still carried that conviction when I met Mark fifteen years later.

"I want to adopt someday," I warned him during our courtship in college.

I don't know that he took me all that seriously—until we had two healthy little girls and began working on behalf of orphans. It was then I started to plead my case. After a length of time, and much determined persistence on my part, Mark agreed to consider it. We attended an information meeting on international adoption at an agency called Bethany Christian Services. Because of our involvement in Africa, we wanted to adopt from there, but to our surprise, Ethiopia was the only African country open for adoption to the United States. After talking and praying about it, it just didn't seem like the right fit for us. We were so invested in South Africa and really wanted to adopt from there. Confused and more than a little disappointed, I wondered what God was doing.

But my disappointment lasted only a short while because I found out I was pregnant. So we put our adoption plan on hold and embraced an unexpected but exciting season.

At the first ultrasound, the technician said, "There are two heartbeats."

*Twins? We're about to have four kids?* Mark and I were shocked. We later learned it was a girl and a boy, and we named them Avery and Walker. The thought of twins—twins!—still overwhelmed us, but we slowly grew used to the idea and started looking forward to how crazy our life was about to be.

At eighteen weeks, I began having contractions. My high-risk-pregnancy doctor put me on medication and strict bed rest. For weeks I had to lie still on the couch as my two busy little girls ran amuck. My family, friends, and neighbors rallied around me, helped with the kids, brought meals, and supported me emotionally, which I desperately needed.

Then at twenty-four weeks, my water broke—in Walker's sac. I was immediately admitted to the hospital, and my doctor told me I would be there, on bed rest and constant monitoring, until the babies were born. The goal was to get me as close to forty weeks as possible.

This was the start of an agonizing time. We celebrated every passing week, because each day was crucial to the development of our babies, but it was hard for me to be away from home, from Mark and my girls, worrying about the twins and feeling helpless. Mark would bring me delicious gourmet cupcakes every Wednesday and light a candle. Once a day, the doctor would allow me twenty minutes outside in a wheelchair to get some fresh air.

One day when I was at twenty-eight weeks, Mark pushed me outside into the July summer heat, and we sat under a big tree in the shade. We blew out the cupcake candle and grinned at each other, thrilled we had made it this far. But that afternoon, I started having regular, intense contractions, each one coming harder and faster. I was in labor. They tried everything to stop it but ended up rushing me into the operating room and performing an emergency C-section.

The operating room was packed with people in blue scrubs and masks, certain doctors and nurses for me and others for Avery and Walker. My nerves were shot, and I was weeping and trembling to the point of nausea. Because of the complications I'd experienced with my epidural for Taylor's delivery, I was petrified to try again.

"Be careful," I warned the anesthesiologist over and over again.

I tried not to shake as he inserted that long needle into my back. A nurse knelt in front of me, and I gripped her hands, pushed my sweaty forehead against hers, and attempted to hold perfectly still as I wept and prayed and pleaded. It took nearly thirty minutes for the anesthesiologist to find the right spot in my spine.

Once they got the epidural going, they had me lie down and began to prepare me for the C-section. Mark's sweet face was right there next to mine as they cut me open. It was the weirdest sensation. There was no pain, but I could feel pressure and my body moving side to side as they stretched my belly open. Panic hit me, and I started screaming and crying as I begged the anesthesiologist for more medicine. He obliged and pretty much knocked me out. After that, I remember only bits and pieces of what happened.

Finally, after what felt like an eternity, I heard a baby crying. It was Avery. A huge team of neonatal doctors and nurses put her in an incubator and rushed her up to the Neonatal Intensive Care Unit on the fifth floor.

Minutes later, they pulled out Walker. But this time, no one said anything and I didn't hear him cry. The silence was like thunder. A team of professionals gathered around him, but they didn't rush him off. Instead, they hovered. They were busy and intent, collaborating quietly as they worked like mad. Then all at once, they bolted out of the room with their hands still busy attending to him in his incubator.

In the recovery room, Mark gently woke me. My mom and dad were there too, just off to the side of my bed. My doctor came in, sat at my right side, and began to speak softly and tenderly to me.

"Avery is fine," he told me. "She's tiny and very sick but stable."

But they weren't sure about Walker. It appeared his lungs had stopped developing at the time of the amniotic rupture. They had an amazing team of specialists working on him and were preparing to fly in another team of doctors and nurses with a rescue medicine.

As the doctor spoke, I kept drifting in and out of consciousness. My eyes didn't want to stay open and my mind refused to focus. In a cloud of confusion, I kept shaking my head and repeating, "I don't understand. I don't understand."

After eight hours and every medical attempt possible to keep Walker alive, the doctors gave us an impossible choice. We had to decide whether or not we would take our son off life support. His underdeveloped lungs could not support the rest of his body, and he was brain dead.

They took me up to see my babies. Wheeling my hospital bed from the second floor to the fifth floor, they pushed me next to the incubators holding my precious little babies. Avery and Walker. Both of them were so small, smaller than any babies I had ever seen. They were covered with cords, wires, and machines, with more machines gathered around them.

The nurses called in a pastor for us, and we had Walker baptized. Pulling a pink curtain around my bed, they removed all the machines, cords, and wires from Walker's gray, one-pound body. I watched as they dressed him in a tiny white outfit, with booties and a cap, and then they handed him to me. He was so small that he fit in the palm of my hand. I held him on my chest, pressed my lips gently to his little head, and sang "Jesus Loves You." Mark wept as he sat there with me, his arms around us both. We cried and prayed, cried and prayed, as our son's heart slowed to a ticking and finally stopped. Walker went right from my hands in that hospital bed directly into the arms of Jesus in heaven.

A nurse tenderly took his little body from me, and as they began to wheel my bed away, I let out a guttural scream and wept until I threw up. They pushed me out of the NICU as I protested, "I can't do this! I can't do this!"

Back in my room, the nurse gave me something that knocked me out. When I woke in the morning, I opened my eyes to see that Mark was right there, sleeping next to me, and I realized it wasn't just a bad dream. It was real. This was my real life—our only son had died. Our daughter would grow up without her twin. I began to sob uncontrollably again and couldn't catch my breath. As I went into a panic, Mark called for the nurses, who tried to console me and then gave me a drug to calm me down. I cried for hours with the covers pulled up over my head.

Mark made all the decisions and arrangements for the funeral, and we buried Walker eight days after he died. We clung to each other during that time and talked about everything at length, leaving no issue unaddressed and crying with each other constantly. Surrounding ourselves with close family and friends, we managed to get through that tragic season as a strong force, something to be reckoned with.

Days and weeks passed. Avery grew bigger and stronger. I spent all day, every day, in the NICU with her, holding her little two-pound body on my chest inside my shirt. My body heat helped regulate her temperature, her heartbeat synched to mine, and an unshakable bond formed between us.

After ten long, emotionally exhausting weeks, Avery was finally ready to go home.

# Seven

## FROM ASHES TO BEAUTY

• • •

As the dust settled, I slowly began to resume my work with Acres of Love. When Avery was eighteen months old, we decided to travel to South Africa as a family. It was incredible to share South Africa and Acres of Love with Mark and the girls and watch them interact with the country, culture, and children I loved so much. Finally, it wasn't just "my thing" but a place and a cause the whole family embraced.

I took my young daughters on the dirt roads in Soweto and watched them hand out biscuits to barefoot, dirty children. I was impressed to see how much they enjoyed interacting with these kids, with no fear or pretense but a deep level of compassion and care. It was a delight to watch my girls having fun with the kids at the Bridges Forever Home. We took everybody out for pizza and ice cream, and they all got along seamlessly. The kids danced to music in the hallways of our hotel, jumped on the trampoline in their backyard, and climbed on the jungle gym. The boys taught Mark how to throw and catch a rugby ball. We held hands as we walked through the zoo together, and one of the young Bridges girls held Avery on her lap while the baby napped. We went to church together, picnicked together, and truly bonded as an extended family.

Upon our return, Mark and I began to revisit the idea of adoption. When I contacted the agency, I was startled to learn they had just opened up adoptions to the U.S. from South Africa and were accepting ten families into a pilot program. We jumped on the opportunity, applied for the program, and were invited to begin the adoption process. In a meeting with our social worker, we discussed the age and gender we wanted, what medical issues we were willing to take on, etc.

"Let's leave the gender and age requirements open," Mark suggested.

We did so—and even reported that we were open to taking siblings. We wanted to let God make the ultimate decision for our family and didn't want to put any of our own perimeters on this. We chose to "let go and let God," as people say.

It took us about nine months to complete all the paperwork, get the finger printing done, collect our letters of recommendation, finish our physicals, do our training hours, complete interviews with our social worker, and have all the paperwork notarized. The night before we sent off our huge pile of official adoption documents to South Africa, we all put our hands on them and prayed.

Then the waiting began. Months passed as we watched the phone and hoped for the call from the agency that would tell us we were matched with a child. I tried to stay busy and trust God to bring us the right child at the perfect time, but it was difficult.

Finally, one early afternoon in May 2013, we got the call. Our family had been matched with a little Zulu boy from just outside of Durban, South Africa. His name was Melokuhle ("Melo"). He was two and a half years old and had been living with his foster parents in a small children's home for eighteen months. They sent us a short medical report and a few pictures—he was gorgeous.

When the agency gave us the go-ahead to fly to South Africa to meet him, we went as a family, all three girls in tow. We were excited and nervous with anticipation about what our little boy was going to be like. Ever since we'd heard about him, I had spent many sleepless nights milling over the same anxious questions: Will he like us? Will we like him? Will his personality fit in with our little family culture? Will he like snuggling on the couch with us when we watch movies? Will he act out? Will he be accepted by our extended family? Friends? Community? Will everyone stare at us everywhere we go? Will people ask awkward questions and make hurtful comments? Is this the right thing to do, both for him and for our girls? Am I really equipped to handle this? Have we made a mistake? Part of me was thrilled. Another part felt terrified.

Finally back in South Africa, we rented a big white van, and Mark nervously drove on the opposite side of the car, on the opposite side of the road, with our family of five to go meet Melo and become a family of six. We made our way in the rain up a very steep, muddy, slippery dirt road to the house where Melo was living.

This was it—the moment we had dreamed about, imagined, and played out in our minds countless times. We saw the house. We saw his foster mom on the front porch holding him. We fumbled over one another trying to get out of the car and up to the house.

There he was.

He was beautiful, small, skinny, and clearly confused and apprehensive. We said our gentle hellos and gave him some time and space to warm up to us. Once inside, we sat on the couch, interacted with the twenty other kids living in the small house, and patiently waited to bond with our boy. It touched my heart to watch our girls play and connect with him. Though Melo seemed shy and overwhelmed at the beginning, he quickly took to our oldest daughter, Katelyn, and it was such a treat to watch them interact and bond.

He slowly came out of his shell. Once the rain cleared, we went outside to play. We gave the kids the biscuits we had brought, and Melo would not stop eating them—he must have had a dozen just by himself. We blew bubbles for the kids to chase (Melo kept trying to drink the mixture out of the bottle) and pushed the kids on the swings, jumped on the trampoline with them, and cheered them on while they rode their little tricycles.

At one point, Melo walked over to me, extended his arms, and motioned for me to pick him up. I held him for a long time, rocking him side to side as he rested his head on my shoulder. I loved everything about this moment, and just as I was thinking my sweet boy was going to fall asleep in my arms, he vomited all those biscuits down my back. I thought, *Yep, I'm his mom.*

The next day, we returned to the small house to take Melo home with us. When we got there, they were bathing him. We brought a brand-new outfit for him and got him dressed. We said our emotional goodbyes to his foster parents and the rest of the kids, buckled little Melo into our big van, and started back down the steep road. He was so quiet. I looked back and saw Avery reach over from her car seat into his and grab his hand. One single tear rolled down his beautiful black cheek.

We spent the next few days at a beachfront hotel in Durban just playing and bonding and getting to know each other. Melo was sweet and loving, smart and playful, active and affectionate. After just a short time, it felt like he had been a part of our family forever. It took five weeks to complete the entire process in South Africa. Between our court appointment, filing paperwork, rushing documents to Home Affairs, and filing for his visa, new birth certificate, and passport, we traveled all around the country and enjoyed our adventure together as a family.

When we returned home to the States, Melo immediately stole the heart of every person who met him. As he blossomed, he became friendly, outgoing, and kind. His adorable South African accent delighted everyone who heard him speak.

For me, the most beautiful part of the transition period was watching him bond with his new sister Avery. With the two of them being so close in age, Mark and I had worried about how she would accept him, and he her. But it was obvious from the beginning that they really liked each other. They got along beautifully, played together all the time, and became the best of friends. Avery flourished in their relationship, thriving in a whole new way, gaining confidence, and learning to adore this little boy she was going to grow up with. She was meant to live life as a twin, purposed to have a brother as her partner. It was like God was replacing something she had lost, and now she was complete. Witnessing the special relationship between little Avery and her newfound brother has proven to be the biggest blessing in this whole journey.

# *Eight*

## PROVISION IS IN THE ASSIGNMENT

• • •

In October 2014, I led another group of women from Southern California to South Africa to visit Acres of Love. This trip was cause for celebration because finally, after eight years, we had secured all the funding for the Bridges Forever Home. We had raised enough support and gathered enough donor partners around us that we were bringing in a sustainable $90,000 a year to take care of the children.

We had a wonderful time in South Africa and even got to take the kids with us on safari for two nights. It was a treat to spoil them, to fill their plates at the lodge buffet, and watch their excitement over zebras, elephants, giraffes, and lions.

On the final night of our trip, we sat out on a restaurant patio and enjoyed a lovely dinner as we debriefed, sharing the lessons we had learned and the impact the children had made on us.

One of the women shared, "While I relish in our accomplishments of providing for one home of children, I can't help but feel like we should be doing more." Orphans wandered the streets right next door to the restaurant where we were sitting.

That evening, we decided that upon our return to the States, we were going to put all our time and energy into raising enough money to open another Acres of Love home, so we could rescue another ten children. We were excited—and nervous. It's a tall task to commit to funding the purchase of a home and then raising an additional $90,000 every subsequent year to care for the children. It didn't take long for us to realize the magnitude of what we had just decided. One by one, the team members started mentioning their inadequacies, all the things they weren't good at, the roadblocks we would inevitably come up against in our efforts to ask people to join us in our mission.

"But, ladies," I said, "remember it isn't us. We aren't the ones who are going to provide for the kids. It's God. If we commit to this assignment to care for orphans and we trust God, He will provide everything to meet our needs. Let's pray about it tonight and revisit the idea in the morning over breakfast."

When I got back to my hotel room, I sent a message to Gerda, excitedly telling her of our plan to raise the funding for another Forever Home. This had been a dream of mine since I first got involved with the organization.

When I woke up the next morning, I had a reply from her. They already had the funding for a new home, she said; they had just purchased it and were in the process of moving six kids in. They were praying and trusting that God would bring someone alongside this home to provide the monthly funding to support the children's everyday needs such as food, clothes, school tuition, medical expenses, therapies, extracurricular activities, etc. Would we be interested in partnering with this new home in the recently expanded Cape Town region?

I couldn't believe it! At breakfast, I told the ladies that God had already provided for us. While we were sleeping, we had received a home and six new kids. All of us were blown away.

This second home would be called Unathi Forever Home. *Unathi* is an Xhosa word that means "God is with us." It was such an incredible example of how God works. We answered His call to care for the "least of these," stepped out in obedience and faith, said yes and trusted that He would provide everything we needed—and then He blessed us, and six orphaned children, beyond measure.

We returned home to Southern California and got busy hosting countless coffees, holiday breakfasts, and dinner parties, inviting everyone we knew to come see the pictures of our trip, hear the stories of our adventure, and learn about Acres of Love and the kids we were so in love with. We shared the miraculous story of the Unathi Forever Home and boldly asked people to commit to giving a minimum of $50 every month in an effort to come alongside the long-term care of these children.

A couple of months into our fundraising efforts, Gerda messaged me that a church in South Africa had committed to partner with us and cover half of the monthly costs to run the home. I was overwhelmed with God's goodness and was so excited to share with the ladies that once again, He was with us and faithfully providing all we needed to take care of these children. In four short months, the Unathi Forever Home was fully funded, and kids were living there. Back in the States, all of us were in awe of the way God had orchestrated everything and allowed us to be a part of it.

# Nine

## WHO ARE WE?

...

"I hadn't planned on asking you this, but would you like to join me on a trip to South Africa in March?"

I was in a meeting with Gerda in our Southern California office when she dropped that question on me out of the blue. Of course I wanted to go, and I invited Sue and Gretchen, two of my closest friends and loyal Acres of Love supporters, to join us.

A short time later, we were on a plane headed back to South Africa. Excited and uncertain at the same time, we kept giggling and asking each other, "Who are we? Who does this? Why are we going back to South Africa again? What is God up to?"

All we knew for sure was that we were willing to go where we sensed God was leading us. We were compelled to follow Him and eager to see what He had in store for us to experience and learn. All three of us had a strong sense that there was more to our involvement with Acres of Love and South Africa. We could have easily focused just on raising support, but something was calling us into a deeper commitment. It was almost like we were traveling through a thick fog;

we couldn't see where we were going or what was in front of us, but we were determined to keep pressing in and moving forward. When opportunities arose, we decided we were going to say yes and walk through all open doors.

God is subtle sometimes. He often speaks in a still, small voice (1 Kings 19:12), and in many cases, His calling isn't loud and obvious and pushy. He doesn't write it in the sky or flash it before us in bright lights. Many times we could easily miss it and talk ourselves out of it, so we have to be committed to leaning in, straining to hear Him, and staying close and connected to Him. When taking those first steps of obedience, we might even wonder, "What in the world is happening right now?" Because we don't see the big picture. Following Christ and learning about our purpose and calling is a relentless pursuit slowly discovered.

Gerda and her husband, Ryan, describe Acres of Love as a "slow and steady work." When they first started out, they didn't know how big it was going to be or the impact it was going to make, but something compelled them. They trusted the Lord and walked in obedience; their faith increased and He provided all they needed.

On this trip, my two friends and I read from *My Utmost for His Highest* by Oswald Chambers, our favorite devotional, every morning over breakfast. One morning we read, "It takes a heart broken by conviction of sin, baptized by the Holy Spirit, and crushed into submission to God's purpose to make a person's life a holy example of God's message."[2] The idea of being "crushed into submission" moved my heart. That's what I felt like was happening to me. I realized that in order to truly follow Christ, I had to lay aside any plans I'd made for my life and surrender it all to the Lord. This required a daily, hourly, moment-by-moment act of submission, recognizing

---

2 Oswald Chambers, *My Utmost for His Highest* (Grand Rapids, MI: Discovery House, 1992).

I was no longer in charge. In a way, it felt like I was being emptied. For me, this became a season of being willing to let go, a process that elevated God in my life. I knew He would rebuild, transform, and use me for His purposes. Even this trip to South Africa was an example of being led. I was acting in obedience and following Him, with no idea of the plan or purpose, but I was walking in faith, trusting that it would all be revealed to me at just the right time. This time in my life was exciting, scary, invigorating, and terrifying.

When Gerda invited me to speak at an Acres of Love staff meeting, I shared about my role in the United States as an emissary and what we were doing to support Acres of Love. The team in South Africa was overwhelmed by our level of involvement. They hadn't realized that so many people on the other side of the world were giving money and praying for the work the staff members were doing with the children every day. It was such an honor to share how God had mobilized us to work together to solve this problem they faced in South Africa. All of us saw at a deeper level how Acres of Love has had a profound ripple effect, touching the lives of people around the globe. Not only were the rescued children being blessed, but so were the donor partners, the staff, the volunteers, and the local community. It was amazing to witness the impact this organization was making, all because one couple had responded to God's call to care for orphans. Ryan and Gerda had said yes, stepped forward in obedience, and trusted the Lord with their lives and plans.

Then came the morning we were sitting at the coffee shop in the Johannesburg airport with Gerda, listening in awe to her stories as we waited to board our flight to Cape Town and visit a few Forever Homes in that region. Gerda told story after story of the miraculous things that had happened in and through Acres of Love: supernatural visitations, financial provision, miraculous healings.

*Why don't more people know about this?* I wondered.

Sue, Gretchen, and I separately but simultaneously had a profound revelation of God that morning. We could clearly see Him moving in and through Gerda's life to touch so many children. This wasn't just a good thing she was doing, some act of charity, but we could really sense God's presence and favor on the whole ministry. Yes, we had already committed ourselves to the organization, and we wanted to be involved, but something totally new was being birthed in us. God touched us in such a powerful way that morning in the airport, and we wanted to know Him more. More than ever, we knew our work with Acres of Love was something He was doing.

"Have you ever thought to document the hundreds of amazing stories you've shared with us over the years?" I asked Gerda. Others needed to have the opportunity to hear what God was doing in and through Acres of Love.

"I've considered it," she answered, "but I've been so busy doing the work that I haven't found the time to write it all down."

It was nearly time for us to board the plane, and we made a last-minute trip to the restroom. In those few moments of privacy, I felt the Lord tell me, "You've always wanted to write a book. You've been waiting for Me to direct you on it. Well, this is it. You will write the stories for Gerda."

I ran out to Gerda and offered to document the stories for her.

"Go for it," she said. "It is delegated!"

# Ten

## FRONT-ROW SEATS

...

Over the next six months, I interviewed Ryan and Gerda weekly, often with Sue and Gretchen sitting beside me. The mornings we spent with them were special times. We knew we were going to hear stories that would reveal God in astounding ways, and all three of us crowded in to know Him better.

Something supernatural was drawing us. We weren't just listening to stories about Acres of Love and the kids they had rescued, but we were in the presence of God in that room as He revealed Himself to us. It became a sacred space. During each interview, a sweet sense of peace, wonder, and awe filled the air as God became more and more visible to us. We were getting to know Him through the stories of what He did and how He moved; it felt like the scales were falling off our eyes. While some of the stories were straight-out miracles and "unbelievable" to the natural mind, we never doubted them for a moment. It was like the Holy Spirit was right beside us to confirm everything we were learning. He put in our hands this precious gift of faith, and we responded in belief. Ryan and Gerda deposited many "seeds" in us. It was a season of invitation, seeking, and discovery.

We learned about their individual journeys of faith, the details of how Acres of Love started, their trials and successes, the stories of the children they rescued, how Ryan and Gerda discovered their assignments, and how they learned to walk in obedience. We felt honored to spend so much time with them, to have a "front-row seat" to the work God was doing in and through their lives.

In getting to know them better, we also were able to know God better. That's the special thing about them and Acres of Love. Their lives are a testimony of Jeremiah 17:8: They are like trees planted along a riverbank, with roots that are not bothered by the heat or worried by the long months of drought. Their leaves stay green, and they never stop producing fruit. Because of the way *they* stayed so close to the Lord, seeking Him constantly and drawing from Him everything they needed to live godly lives and care for the children, I found myself on a journey to know God the way they knew Him. I wanted the kind of faith they possessed and to make the impact they were making. I wanted my life to be completely committed to the Lord and His purpose and plan. Just as Ryan and Gerda were, I wanted to be a vessel, a steward of the Lord's presence, so He could fill me and flow through me to others. I wanted to be like them: to believe God and act like it.

What would that look like in my life?

## • WHAT IF? •

I know that God brought Ryan and Gerda into my life to show me what it looks like to believe everything He says in His Word and act like it, every single day, in everything I do.

What would happen in the world if every believer in Jesus lived that way? Obviously, it won't look the same for everyone. We won't all rescue orphans in Africa like Ryan and Gerda do. We are in different places and circumstances, and we've all been given unique gifts and talents.

But what would that level of faith and obedience look like for me? I really wanted to find out.

# Part Two

## RYAN AND GERDA

. . .

# Eleven

## GERDA

...

Lena worked on a large family farm in western Transvaal, South Africa, that had been in an Afrikaans family for generations. She was a domestic worker, as were many blacks during the apartheid era in South Africa. A strikingly beautiful, dignified African woman, she would start her day's work early in the morning before the sun came up.

She lived in a mud hut, set off and away from the manor house. It was dark and damp inside, and the hut's floors were made of mud and cow manure. Life was simple; she didn't have much but everything was kept very neat. There were just a few shelves on the wall. Out of newspaper she made lace that would go underneath her cups. She had eight children and her babies didn't wear diapers. She loved having a big family and always prayed she would have another baby. Cooking for her children in three black pots over a fire outside the house, she often made a dish called pap, which is flour boiled in water. She lived with such dignity, did her work with pride, and took care of her family with love.

The farm owner's granddaughter used to come for weeks at a time to stay on the farm. Mesmerized by Lena, she would follow her around all day and talk with her. She helped Lena with her work around the farm and admired Lena's long, dark arms as she washed the clothes and hung them on the line to dry. In the evenings, she would follow Lena home and play with her children. The little girl admired the pride Lena took in her simple life. While she didn't have much, she seemed to have everything. That little girl was Gerda.

"I think she showed me the beauty and strength in a woman," Gerda told me. "Her circumstances, education, and possessions did not define her. Her strength was in her confidence as a woman; her joy was in simple things. She had the whitest teeth, a tall, slender neck, and a ready smile. And she listened. Even when my grandma was mean or her husband unfaithful, she was above her circumstances. Life is for the brave.

"I will never forget how amazing she was and her recovery after every baby. She carried them on her back: bare-bottom, bonny babies with the most gorgeous color skin, smooth ebony and soft." Lena worked hard and with excellence.

"I think God has always allowed me to see everyone the same," Gerda said. She used to work in South Africa with a large film company and many celebrities, and she could never understand why anyone wanted an autograph. "We are all the same. Even today I love to see the 'little people' in others' eyes but great in God's eyes. The Kingdom of God is different to the world. The least will be the greatest. So on the red carpet of heaven will be the orphans we are taking care of at Acres of Love. We are entertaining angels."

I've had the privilege of spending a lot of time with Gerda over the last ten years. We've had countless meetings in the Acres of Love office in Southern California; we've traveled to South Africa together, shared delicious dinners with our husbands, and spoken daily about God and His Word and our passion for the children we care for.

As Gerda speaks with the beautiful accent of her homeland, her voice is gentle and compassionate but commanding, and I find myself hanging on her every word. This book exists in part because of her. I became willing to believe in God for miracles because I had seen what He was doing through her family and ministry. And it all started on a farm in South Africa.

# Twelve

## GARETH

...

In the beginning, Ryan and Gerda loved that house. Bright purple jacaranda trees lined the street, and a little creek ran through their backyard. Back then they lived in this perfect little world, and it seemed as though everything happened their way. An amazing couple, they had a romantic courtship, were wildly successful in business, and enjoyed the finer things in life. Everything was ideal. Sundays were their favorite day of the week because after church, they would go home and prepare a leg of lamb, and family would come over and friends would stop by. They always had a cake ready because they never knew who was going to come over and visit. They lingered out in the backyard for hours with their loved ones until the sun went down.

But that was then. Gerda grew to hate that house and eventually told Ryan just to give it away. It reminded her of all the lonely months she had spent locked away trying to keep their second son, Gareth, alive. She had gone into labor at thirty-four weeks. At first, Gareth seemed perfectly healthy, but at his first checkup, they had to wait for hours in a tiny, inconvenient sitting room, and Gareth began to grow increasingly irritable. Eventually he started screaming and wouldn't nurse. By the time they were called back to see the pediatrician, they discovered little Gareth had a strangulated hernia from all the screaming and needed surgery right away.

The surgery that should have taken thirty minutes instead took hours. When Gareth was finally wheeled out in an incubator, a team of nurses surrounded him. The doctor told Ryan and Gerda that at one point, they hadn't been able to resuscitate him. He stayed in the hospital for a few days, and when they were able to bring him home, Gerda couldn't feed him; he could hardly suck. For weeks and weeks, she tried every two hours and was able to get only a couple of ounces of fluid into him.

"It was such an awful time," Gerda told me. "I think the Lord showed me then what families go through in South Africa and what these children go through. We knew so many people and yet nobody came and visited [during our time of hardship]. It was as if he was never born. It was the most heartbreaking thing. We were in this church that really was teaching about faith, and it was almost like the enemy was saying, 'You've done something wrong!' But I'm thinking that the Lord had such an amazing plan for all of it.

"I remember we used to just kneel by Gareth's bed and say, 'Lord, we thank You that Gareth can drink his bottle.' We thanked Him for every little success. We prayed every day that he would be able to crawl, that he would be able to walk.

"All of a sudden, this incredible loneliness and isolation set in—the shame because people wouldn't even use 'special needs.' They would use awful words, how they would explain children. And I never understood it. There is no support—at all—when you go through that. There isn't support from clinic. It's just like all of a sudden, you are all alone."

Today, when Acres of Love receives a child with special needs, it means a lot to her. "Shaka was locked in a box because his family didn't want him. Children are dying. Funani was left in hospital. Anele wasn't even bathed by the nursing staff because she is special needs; she has clubbed feet. Just think how horrific that rejection is." Gerda added, "Maybe right there God called us."

About Gareth, she said, "I just wanted to protect him from the world, from someone not loving him. I think sometimes you have to go through that pain to know the compassion that you need."

Ryan and Gerda moved out and eventually used that home as the office for Acres of Love. The social worker's office was set up in Gareth's old room. Every phone call for every baby who came in was taken in that room, in the exact spot where his crib used to be.

"That gave me the courage to say yes for every special needs child," Gerda said.

# Thirteen

## DISCOVERING THE ASSIGNMENT

• • •

When God called them, Ryan and Gerda were focused on raising their four children and growing their business. Ryan qualified for the Million Dollar Round Table, which represented 1 percent of all financial advisors in the world. On a regular basis, he was exposed to a lot of creative ideas and successful people.

One day Gerda looked at him and said, "Love, I just don't believe God has blessed us so much in business, and in the knowledge that we have of the Word, and this is it. That we are going to just talk with our friends about the next December holiday, the next overseas trip, our next home alteration, our kids' next private school and where they are going to college. Surely there is more."

In 1994, a move of God began in South Africa—and in Ryan and Gerda. Rodney Howard-Browne, a South African man, was leading revivals all around the world, and God did incredible work in and through him; he was speaking to stadiums full of people. Gerda was asked to organize one of these meetings at the World Trade Center in South Africa, and 22,000 people attended, all by word of mouth.

She and her team were later invited to organize a meeting in Singapore. At the meeting, they were instructed to pray for the people around them, and as Gerda prayed with her group, the others laid hands on her and said, "That which lies before you that looks like a mountain will be like an easy road."

That night, the Holy Spirit's presence felt like a blanket. People sobbed as they were restored, healed, and set free. The Lord birthed something amazing in Ryan and Gerda through these meetings; He burned off "the dross," as Proverbs 25:4 (NIV) says. Letting go of the things that hindered them, they began to pray, "Lord, use our lives!"

As they prayed this prayer, Ryan and Gerda began to notice of the number of orphans around them. They and many of their peers had considered the poverty in South Africa to be a "township problem." It was possible for the well-to-do to leave their beautiful homes, safe and secure behind the standard ten-foot walls with barbed wire and security cameras, and drive to their children's private school and back again, all the while completely oblivious to the real needs of the poor around them. But now Ryan and Gerda looked around with brand-new eyes. They *noticed* the poor; they were troubled by the needy and heartbroken at the sight of children wandering the streets. They started to ask, "Why is the government not doing anything about the orphan crisis? Why isn't the church doing anything?"

They felt the Lord softly reply, "Well, what are you doing about it?"

At the time, Gerda was reading a book called *Acres of Diamonds* by Russell Conwell,[3] who was the founder of Temple University. People called him the "penniless millionaire." His classic "Acres of

---

3 Originally published by John Y. Huber Company of Philadelphia in 1890.

Diamonds" message challenged people to find true wealth right in their backyards. He taught that you don't need to look elsewhere for opportunity, achievement, or fortune; you don't need to run around trying to find resources out in the world because when God gives you an assignment, the resources are right where you are.

A doctor who was in Conwell's congregation took a sick woman to see him, explaining they couldn't find a hospital she could afford. Conwell instructed him to take the upstairs bedroom in his house, and he hired a nurse to treat her. That became Conwell's "hospital." Ryan and Gerda were profoundly moved by this revolutionary concept of using what you already had to solve the problem God placed in front of you.

It was clear that right in their own backyard, in the country they loved so much, there was a massive need. Though many abandoned, desperate children were wandering the streets, no one was doing anything about it. Ryan and Gerda knew they didn't have all the answers or the solutions to the problems that surrounded them; they didn't know how the whole thing was going to play out. But they believed the Lord had called them to do something about these kids, so they decided just to start.

Gerda suggested they take the extra house they owned and get involved. They quickly obtained their license to bring in children, and they dedicated their old house to the Lord in August 1998.

Their first kids came from a hospital about two hours away. They picked up six orphaned children who had been abandoned there and drove home with them on their laps. Even their oldest son, Darren, who was sixteen years old at the time, rode home holding babies. It was a family commitment; they were all in.

When they reached the house, they sat with all the babies, these tiny kids who were sick, desperate, crying, hungry, and in need of baths and clean nappies, and they looked at one another and wondered, "Now what? How did we get here?"

They had prayed that God would use their lives, and when He gave them an assignment, they said yes, knowing the burden He'd put on their hearts. Noticing a need around them, they were willing and available to step in and do the work. Now they were sitting there with six babies who depended on them for everything. Ryan and Gerda didn't know what the next day or next week held and had no idea where their efforts would lead them. They just did the next right thing.

# Fourteen

## BAPTISM BY FIRE

. . .

A missionary friend once told Ryan and Gerda, "That which God calls you to, He will baptize in fire."

It was now December 1998, and more children had come home to Acres of Love. Ryan was closing the year with his business while Gerda organized a big church conference in Cape Town. After going through a difficult battle with the court system, they invited their close friends to stay with them on a wine farm in Stellenbosch for Christmas. They were looking forward to a relaxing holiday with their family and friends as they marinated in Jesus' love and celebrated His birth.

One afternoon they went for a leisurely walk across the farm. As they picked raspberries and enjoyed the beautiful scenery, they recalled all they had recently been through and praised God for His goodness. As they approached the farmhouse with full baskets, they saw their nanny, Lala, waving her arms and motioning for them to come quickly. Darren had fallen off his bike and had a huge gash on his knee. Gerda silently prayed, *Lord, can we just have a reprieve?* We are so tired! They called the owner of the home and asked about the best place to take Darren. The owner confidently recommended Stellenbosch Mediclinic, where Darren received great assistance. All bandaged up, he returned to the farm.

Two days later, the morning after Christmas, they went horseback riding in Franschhoek. Ryan, who wasn't experienced with horses, ended up with the owner's horse, a cross-country champion. The owner told Ryan, "Just hold him tight because he wants to run!" He helped Ryan get situated but forgot to adjust the stirrups for him.

The nine of them rode up the mountain, and on the way back, Ryan continued on ahead. A short time later, Gerda spotted a young farm boy running to them through the trees.

"Terrible accident!" he yelled. "Terrible accident!"

Ryan's horse had taken off. Slipping on the dewy cobblestones, it had slammed Ryan's leg against a wall and then jumped over the wall, which was ten feet high. Ryan went sailing through the air with the horse and fell to the ground. When Gerda and the others reached him, he could hardly breathe. He had back injuries; his ribs pierced his lungs, causing them to burst; and his diaphragm had collapsed. Gerda called for an ambulance. When the paramedics arrived, they retrieved a piece of plank, put Ryan on it, and said they would take him to a local state hospital.

"No," Gerda protested. "You will take him to Stellenbosch Mediclinic!"

The ambulance driver refused because it was out of their jurisdiction, but because Gerda had just been there with Darren, she knew Stellenbosch Mediclinic was a good hospital. When she called and told them her husband had suffered a terrible riding accident, they sent their own paramedic to fetch Ryan.

Nine doctors at the clinic were just finishing their rounds when the ambulance arrived with Ryan, and they all stayed to work on him. They resuscitated him in ICU. Gerda remembers just standing there as people ran back and forth past her, and no one would tell her anything about her husband.

Finally a redheaded doctor came out and said, "Mrs. Audagnotti, your husband has had fatal injuries. He's not going to live."

In the aftermath of this horrific pronouncement, some of Ryan and Gerda's closest friends called and said that God had given them a Scripture to share with her. One passage was Isaiah 58:6–9:

> *No, this is the kind of fasting I want:*
> *Free those who are wrongly imprisoned;*
> *lighten the burden of those who work for you.*
> *Let the oppressed go free,*
> *and remove the chains that bind people.*
> *Share your food with the hungry,*
> *and give shelter to the homeless.*
> *Give clothes to those who need them,*
> *and do not hide from relatives who need your help.*
> *Then your salvation will come like the dawn,*
> *and your wounds will quickly heal.*
> *Your godliness will lead you forward,*
> *and the glory of the LORD will protect you from behind.*
> *Then when you call, the LORD will answer.*
> *"Yes, I am here," he will quickly reply.*

The other passage was Psalm 41:1–3:

> *Oh, the joys of those who are kind to the poor!*
> *The LORD rescues them when they are in trouble.*
> *The LORD protects them*
> *and keeps them alive.*
> *He gives them prosperity in the land*
> *and rescues them from their enemies.*

*The LORD nurses them when they are sick*
*and restores them to health.*

Gerda took these Scriptures to Ryan and said to him, "Love, what happened is you had an accident, but I want to read you these Scriptures, and we are going to trust God, because we can stand on the Word." She was very careful about the words she used when she spoke to him and was protective about who she let see him, how they reacted and what they said. Shielding him from negative words, she spoke only life to him, declaring God's Word. She trusted what the Bible said and had faith for his healing. She believed what God had said and acted like it.

The Lord's presence was in that hospital room, so tangible she could feel it. On Sunday night, Ryan couldn't speak because he was on a ventilator, but he wrote down what he wanted to say and used his pet name for Gerda: "Lady, Jesus sat at the end of my bed. He reached His hand out to me and He said, 'You're behind schedule. But I have a plan for your life. I'll make up the time. You'll be fine.'" It was like Jesus was dressed in glory, as if he wore illuminated light.

The next morning Ryan wrote to Gerda again. This time he said, "Don't leave me today, Lady." That afternoon the nurses came in to wash him and asked Gerda to leave the room. She went down the hall with Darren to grab a cup of tea. As she took the cup in her hand, she remembered what Ryan had written to her. She ran back to the room and saw he wasn't breathing. His eyes wide open, the monitors were going off as two ICU nurses worked on him. Gerda ran out of the room and screamed down the hallways for help. They got the doctors out of surgery, and the hospital psychiatrist grabbed Gerda and pushed her into the next room. Through the window, she could see the monitors, which told her the news wasn't good.

Blood or a piece of injured lung had clogged up the ventilator so Ryan couldn't breathe. They had to sedate him. Every ten minutes, they would put saline down into his lungs and then suction it out to make sure his airway was clear. It was awful for Gerda to watch him go through this because it was like he was drowning.

He could no longer write, so Gerda would sit there and just talk to him. She would read the Bible to him and remind him that they were trusting God and Ryan was going to be healed.

When Ryan improved and they finally took him off the ventilator, Gerda told him, "I know you have always had a dream of moving to America. I will do your dream. We have to go!"

Within a few months, Ryan had recovered and they left South Africa for Southern California, where they continued running Acres of Love. Gerda was involved in every detail, working tirelessly with the amazing staff they had in place in South Africa. Since their move, she has spent a couple of weeks in South Africa every two months. Acres of Love began to form amazing relationships with people in the United States and all over the world who learned about the work they were doing and wanted to get involved as committed donor partners. They have grown the organization carefully and intentionally, never wanting to expand just for the sake of growth but only as the Lord leads.

Since its birth in 1998, Acres of Love has grown to own and operate thirty Forever Homes in both Johannesburg and Cape Town. It sets the standard for orphan care in the world and continues to rescue and care for the most vulnerable children in South Africa. They have looked after approximately six hundred children over the twenty years they've been in operation. Every child comes in with a unique and heartbreaking story, and the staff members dedicate each of these precious kids to the Lord and bring them into a home filled with mercy and grace.

Here are some of the children's stories.

# Part Three

## THE CHILDREN

...

# fifteen

## SOLOMON

• • •

Solomon was one of the first babies Acres of Love took in. His admission report showed that he was HIV positive. While it is the goal to have as many children adopted from Acres of Love as possible, they knew it was unlikely that Solomon would be adopted because of his diagnosis. Most people don't want to take in a child who is so sick or whose needs will be an ongoing financial burden.

One day a missionary friend came to the Acres of Love house to lay hands on and pray for all of the HIV-positive kids. When another blood test was done, staff members discovered that little Solomon was negative for HIV. When the social worker found out he'd tested negative, she said he needed to be adopted.

At Christmas time, they asked Solomon what he wanted for Christmas. His response came easily: "An umbrella, a flute, and a mommy and a daddy!" Soon after, the social worker said she'd found a match for Solomon. It was a woman who lived in a squatter camp and sold secondhand clothing in the streets. Gerda said she wasn't comfortable with that because she couldn't see how it was in Solomon's best interest to be sent back to that kind of situation after he'd spent the last two years in a beautiful, safe home. It wouldn't be right to send him back to live in a squatter camp where he would spend his days sitting by his mother who was selling old clothes to make a living.

Gerda involved her attorney in the situation because it wasn't a good match. The child protective organization said that they would hold back, but they wanted the adoption agency that Acres of Love worked with to find a local family to adopt him within six weeks.

Ryan and Gerda began diligently praying. On December 20, they received a call from a local couple. The husband was a pastor and they had biological sons. They wondered if there was a child at Acres of Love who had asked for a mommy and daddy for Christmas, because they thought it would be nice to bring that child into their home just for Christmas and bless them. They didn't intend to adopt. So Solomon went with them just for the holiday, but they fell in love with him and were so moved by his story that they decided to make him a permanent member of their family.

Here was a child abandoned in a rural hospital. He was HIV positive, suffering from a disease that has no cure. No one wanted him. He was utterly alone and forgotten, and his future looked bleak. How could he possibly escape this hopeless situation?

But hours away from that hospital, in a bustling city of affluence and opportunity, God put His hand on a couple and began to work in their hearts. They took notice of the orphan crisis happening around them and remembered what the Word of God said about His heart for the "least of these." Responding to His call, they engaged His plan, and their act of obedience changed this little boy's life. They literally rescued him out of darkness and brought him into light. Not only was he healed of this "incurable" disease, but as people in the community took notice of Acres of Love, they, too, responded to God's call and offered to get involved. A family fell in love with this little boy, and his story radically changed—because Ryan and Gerda chose to believe God and trust Him. Their actions reflected their faith.

# Sixteen

## AYANDA

...

Richard was an ex-South African living in Orange County, California. A successful businessman, he contacted Gerda and said he had money in a savings account that he wanted to donate to open a new house. He traveled back to South Africa and told his sister-in-law, Angie, that he was going to get involved with Acres of Love. She was a volunteer at a nearby orphanage and thought it was ridiculous to give that much money to help just a few children. She felt it would be more useful to spread the money around to help greater numbers.

But one day at the orphanage where she volunteered, she found a baby lying dead in its crib and nobody even knew. The orphan problem was so immense that organizations with good intentions found themselves inundated. Overwhelmed and underfunded, they took in as many kids as they could and, in the process, lost the ability to pay attention to the details. After this experience, Angie became very passionate about the cause and began to volunteer at Acres of Love. She encouraged Richard to buy a home in the east region where she lived, so she could be highly involved. She helped purchase the home, equip it, and hire the house mom.

When Acres of Love first started taking in abandoned and HIV-positive children, pediatric antiretroviral medications didn't exist. But then Dr. Leon Levin, a Hasidic Jewish man, had a breakthrough with the medications and began teaching all over the country. He was very knowledgeable on the topic and introduced the treatment with babies. Angie had an excellent rapport with Dr. Levin because he was her children's pediatrician. When they opened this new Forever Home in the east region, they decided to house their sickest HIV-positive children there, so they could be close to Dr. Levin. The children who went into that home were on the brink of death. Angie and her husband, Noel, became intimately involved with these kids and were very hands-on with them.

A few months after the home opened, the children were finally settling in with their house mom, and Acres of Love invited Richard back to South Africa for a dedication ceremony, where they would give thanks to God for His provision and commit the children into His care. During the ceremony, they received a phone call from the Acres of Love office letting them know they had a new little girl for admission to the home. They were still on the front lawn enjoying the ceremony when a social worker pulled up in a flatbed truck with Ayanda sitting in the back all by herself. A skinny little thing, she was wearing a bright yellow shirt and had a big bump on her forehead. When they asked about it, the social worker said the girl had hit her head. However, when they bathed her later that day, they realized she had bumps all over her body.

The house mom recalls, "Ayanda had been staying with her father and stepmother after the passing of her mother. She was severely abused by her stepmother, who would lock her out of the house with her baby sister in the cold winter nights while [the stepmother] would go out boozing." Ayanda went without food and became very sick, with lumps and sores all over her body. "Her baby sister was

Ayanda's responsibility because she was supposed to bathe her and do the laundry."

Ayanda and her sister had to rely on the community for shelter, food, and medical care. She wasn't supposed to tell people if she was sick, and if she did, her parents would beat her when she returned home. This kept happening until the teacher who always took Ayanda to the clinic reported the situation to the social worker. Ayanda was worried about her baby sister, and unfortunately, the younger girl passed away before child protective services could save her from the abuse.

Right away, Angie took Ayanda to Dr. Levin, and when the test results came back, they realized she had full-blown AIDS that had already spread to her brain. She also had kaposi sarcoma, a type of cancer that was not curable. They immediately started her on the antiretroviral medications, or ARVs. As was customary in those early days of the ARV treatment, every virus that had been lying dormant in Ayanda's system flared up, and she became very ill. Dr. Levin referred her to a pediatric oncologist. Normally they wouldn't put a child with full-blown AIDS on chemo because it's expensive and the survival rates are so low, but Dr. Levin told Angie, "I have seen so many miracles at Acres of Love. Let's just do it."

So Ayanda began her chemo treatments. After her third round, she grew worse. She was extremely weak, and her hair started to fall out. Gerda, who had been communicating back and forth with the team in South Africa, knew Ayanda was not doing well.

"It was very heartbreaking because the way she was so sick," the house mom said. "I would literally break down and cry most of the time. Each time when the pain came, she would call the name of Jesus. Then I would know she was in pain. Those were the hardest days of my life, spending sleepless nights. There was a time when I really wanted to say, 'We must pray that God must take Ayanda home,' 'cause every day was a struggle."

Angie's husband emailed Gerda on Saturday, November 5, 2005, in the morning. In her kitchen in the United States, Gerda read:

*I greet you all in the name of our Lord and Savior Jesus Christ.*

*It is with much sadness that I tell you that our precious little Ayanda has had a turn for the worst.*

*The doctor phoned this morning to say that Ayanda's pain levels were so high that he had no choice but to treat with morphine. He said that he did not expect her to live much longer and that she was asking for Angie. Angie has picked up the house mom and they are at the hospital at present. I spoke with Angie a couple of minutes ago and Ayanda had had a fit. Her heart rate has slowed to a ticking. Basically, she is out of it and not responsive because of the morphine. The sadness is overwhelming after the somewhat positive news of a couple of days ago.*

*Please pray for the Lord's grace upon her little life, that He would see fit to take away this terrible suffering. Please pray for our baby and for Angie and the house mom and Ayanda's brothers and sisters at home.*

*Love to all*

Gerda was having breakfast with her family when she called Angie in South Africa. The team was all at the hospital with Ayanda. When she got off the phone, Gerda told Ryan that this was going to be so hard on the team and she needed to go be with them. She booked a flight out of Los Angeles that night.

As she sat on the plane waiting for her flight to leave, she felt the Lord say to her, "I didn't send Ayanda to Acres of Love to die but to live. Cancer is a name that has to bow to the name of Jesus. Go lay hands on her."

When Gerda arrived in South Africa on Monday morning, she rushed to the hospital to see Ayanda and reached the hospital around 11. As she walked down the long hallway, she saw Angie with the house mom, who was crying. Ayanda was alone in her room, and Gerda could hear her wailing—a deep, injured, tortured groaning. When the doctor arrived to speak with Angie and the house mom, Gerda stepped away into Ayanda's room. She stood beside her bed, reached out, and laid her hands on the little girl.

"Ayanda, in Jesus' name, you will live and not die. Cancer, you are a name that must bow to the name of Jesus."

Gerda felt nothing in that moment. She didn't get chills or warm fuzzies or feel any kind of reaction whatsoever. Though she didn't notice anything happening with Ayanda, she knew she had done what God had told her to do. She sent everyone home so they could rest, shower, and then bring the other kids to visit their sister.

The nurse told Gerda she was going to wash Ayanda and give her more morphine. So Gerda went to grab a cup of tea and quickly run by the nearby Acres of Love office. She returned a couple of hours later, around 3 p.m. When she walked into the hospital room, she saw that Ayanda was sitting upright in the bed, her eyes wide open as she flicked through the television channels. The nurse reported that the little girl had drunk some juice and eaten a yogurt.

They discharged her two days later.

Angie later told Gerda that while Ayanda lay dying in the hospital, people walked up and down the hallways interceding on her behalf. Angie didn't recognize any of them, so she assumed some were likely nurses. But then one of the nurses came up to Angie and asked her about the man who would come in the middle of the night and hold Ayanda on his lap. They all wanted to know who the man was and thought maybe he worked for Acres of Love. The organization didn't employ any men at that time, and they hadn't sent anyone to sit with her. Was it an angel? Was it Jesus Himself? To this day, none of us know, but clearly God was with this precious little child, protecting her and comforting her. It became obvious that God had a plan for her life.

In January, Acres of Love enrolled Ayanda in school. She was so excited because she'd been watching all the other children get ready in the morning and wanted to be "normal" like they were. They had trouble finding a skirt for her to wear because she was so thin, and she still didn't have any hair. Feeling very protective of her, Angie and the house mom were concerned about how the students and teachers would treat her. They prayed and prayed about this.

When Ayanda walked into her classroom for the first time, Angie asked the teacher to look after her closely, because she had just gone through chemo. The teacher knelt down beside Ayanda and took the scarf off of her own head to show Ayanda that she didn't have any hair either, because she also had just gone through chemo. She hugged Ayanda and told her, "Me and you will do this year together."

Ayanda struggled greatly with her schoolwork that year. She ended up needing to do the year over, which meant she was able to stay with the same teacher. They became very close, and to this day, they still visit each other frequently.

In the end, Ayanda needed only three of the ten chemo treatments and today is completely cancer free. She is on minimal ARVs as the HIV is undetectable in her body. She is one of the few known survivors in the world of both stage four cancer and full-blown AIDS.

Angie wrote in an email to Gerda:

*We so often talk about those early days. We really didn't know what we were taking on. It was just so exciting when we bought the house and then to decorate it and make it look perfect. We were so excited. We made their beds that first day and then sat and waited for Inny to arrive with the children. Nothing could have prepared us for what was going to come. Thando with pneumonia, Amahle so delayed, Siynada like a little skeleton, Kagiso cried non-stop for a year. We didn't know he had fetal alcohol syndrome and then our special Ayanda arrived with that big lump on her head. Inny laid all those ARVs on the kitchen table, gave us a hug and left :) The house mom went into the bathroom and didn't come out for half an hour (she said she was praying) and I was trying to stop Thando from shivering out of her shoes. All the babies were crying and it was time to give them their ARVs and we didn't even know where to start. I phoned Noel and we took Thando to the hospital in Rivonia where they told us she had double pneumonia. We got back to the house at about eleven that night and the house mom had just got Amahle and Siynada to sleep. She then told me about Thando's warts and Siynada's bum (she didn't have any skin on it). We got Thando into bed and left the house at about 2 in the morning . . . and that was the first day!!!! . . . I was back at 8 the next morning and the house mom hadn't slept a wink. For two years we had many days like the first day but we relied totally on God for strength and we prayed and prayed and prayed some more that our children would be healed. I can't believe the miracles that He performed and His total faithfulness.*

# Seventeen

## SHAKA

...

Nine-year-old Shaka lived in a horrible situation in a local township. He had cerebral palsy, and his family treated him very poorly, putting him through horrendous abuse because of his special needs. His grandmother literally kept him locked in a box. He was still in diapers when he arrived at Acres of Love, and his muscles were so weak that he could only crawl. When the Acres of Love team read his report, they were concerned that they wouldn't be able to properly care for him, but one of the social workers said to Gerda, "Imagine what will happen to him if we don't!" They decided to welcome Shaka and trust God for every bit of provision they needed to meet his extensive needs.

Shaka was so traumatized that he didn't do well in enclosed spaces. He is now twenty years old and is still triggered by closed doors, but after so many years of constant care and compassion, he has grown into a beautiful, gentle young man. He will require care throughout his adult life, and Acres of Love will be able to meet his needs at their Special Needs Advancement Center in Cape Town. He has a daily schedule that allows him to be outdoors, helping in the garden and the chicken coop. Wide-open spaces and a consistent routine are helping Shaka heal, and he has truly begun to thrive.

Since taking him in and seeing how well God provided for every one of his needs, Acres of Love has felt more confident in their ability to care for children with special needs. They know that God's provision is wrapped up in His assignments, and their level of care is setting the bar for orphan care in South Africa.

# Eighteen

## THANDIE

...

Thandie was living in a tiny shack with her mother and stepfather, who was an alcoholic and would abuse Thandie terribly when her mother wasn't around. One day when Thandie was about ten years old, she came home early from school. Her mother wasn't there and her stepfather was drunk. He poured gasoline all over her, lit her on fire, and then locked her in the shack. She fought to get out as her body burned. Breaking a window, she climbed out and ran around frantically, screaming in pain. Neighbors came to her rescue. They pushed her down onto the dirt road and tried to get the fire out as her clothes melted into her skin. They put her in a wheelbarrow and walked for miles to get her medical help.

Hours later, she was admitted to the hospital with burn wounds over 80 percent of her body. She remained in the hospital for a long time, and in terrible pain, she would push the call button throughout the night, begging for someone to come and do something to help her, but they ignored her. Her mother and stepfather came one time to see her, and her stepfather laughed. Thandie was eventually released from the hospital and went back to live with them.

A boy named Nelson who lived at one of the Acres of Love homes went to the same community school as Thandie. The principal knew about Thandie's situation and asked Acres of Love if they could do anything to help her.

"Thandie is living in a squatter camp with terrible wounds," he told them. Her mother wasn't capable of getting her back to the hospital, so her wounds weren't being treated properly. She had developed significant scar tissue, so much so that she couldn't bend one arm or leg properly, forcing her to drag her leg behind her. The kids teased her relentlessly and called her "monkey."

Acres of Love was able to rescue Thandie. She underwent several surgeries to remove the scar tissue, and she received all the proper creams to help with her healing. She missed several years of schooling, but at twenty-one years old, she graduated from high school and is interested in the booming field of hospitality in South Africa. She completed a national qualification in food and beverage services and has been granted the opportunity to work at a top hotel.

I had dinner with Thandie a couple of years ago when I was visiting South Africa. This young woman is stunning; she is absolutely gorgeous. Poised, elegant, confident, and mature, she bravely told me the tragic story of her childhood in great detail. She talked about how fortunate she was to be a part of her family at Acres of Love and how special her relationship with Gerda was. Explaining that God had healed her heart, she told me that she had forgiven her mother and stepfather. She feels called to share her story and hopes to travel and bless others with her testimony and message of forgiveness.

I can't help but think of what her life would be like if Acres of Love hadn't taken her in, committed to her, provided the medical and cosmetic care that she received, saturated her with the love of Jesus, and provided her with a faithful family to raise her. Now God can use her life to teach others about who He is, how He loves, and how His followers are His hands and feet sent out into the world.

Thandie recently shared these thoughts with her local church: "Even though my life started with hardship, God gave me a good home. Even though doctors had given up on me and thought I would die, God's grace and healing is bigger than any of them."

As I work with Acres of Love, every time I am able to watch the older children reflect on their life experiences and I see grace and healing woven in the pain, I understand even more that our work is slow and steady as we offer a long-term solution to every child in our care.

# Nineteen

## AMAHLE

•••

Amahle's mother gave birth to her all alone in an open field. For reasons we will never know or understand, she laid tiny Amahle right there in the dirt and left her. Maybe the mother was poor and couldn't care for her. Maybe she was sick with AIDS and knew she was going to die. It's hard to grasp how any mother could abandon her own baby, yet a horrible curse of poverty grips generations of people in South Africa. I find I can have compassion on a woman who is so desperate that she feels abandoning her child is her only option.

When Amahle was found, her umbilical cord was still attached. She was covered in insects, and rodents were busily chewing off her right ear. At Acres of Love, doctors told the staff she wouldn't live because she was severely malnourished and had failure to thrive. They said she would never crawl, never walk, and never talk. The staff placed her in the committed care of her house mom in one of the Forever Homes.

Our team loved her, believed in her, pushed her, and prayed for her. She began to develop—very slowly, but she made progress. Today, contrary to what doctors first said, she walks, runs, and plays. Though she can hear perfectly, her ear lobe looked deformed because of what happened to her in the field. Kids teased her at school, and she began to feel insecure. She always wanted to wear her hair down, strategically placed over her ear to cover it.

When she was about ten years old, she had surgery to attach a prosthetic ear. Acres of Love felt it was important for her to feel good about herself and have confidence. Staff members didn't want her to be ashamed of her ear and be mistreated just because of the way it looked.

I was in South Africa and was able to spend time with Amahle about two months after she received her prosthetic ear. It looked amazing and she was so proud of it. She even had her ears pierced and was so excited to show me the little gold hoop earrings hanging from both of her beautiful ears. She now wears her hair in braids, all pulled up into a bun to show off her ear. She was giddy and smiley as I admired her, and it was wonderful to see how a small cosmetic improvement has given her self-esteem a powerful boost.

I am honored to be a part of an organization that truly meets the complex needs of every child. Our donor support is so amazing that we can go the extra mile, just like we would for our own children, to ensure that each thrives and not just survives. Amahle is now thirteen years old and developmentally delayed, but she's physically strong, healthy, and happy.

When I think of Amahle, Psalm 113:5–8 comes to mind:

*Who can be compared with the LORD our God,*
*who is enthroned on high?*
*He stoops to look down*
*on heaven and earth.*
*He lifts the poor from the dust*
*and the needy from the garbage dump.*

*He sets them among princes,*
*even the princes of his own people.*

Our God, the King of Kings, is active. He pursues and He is engaged. He gets down off of His heavenly throne to look on His people; He stoops, maybe even bending down to get on His knees. For me, this posture shows such concern and humility, that He would go to such efforts to see His people. He scours the earth to find the poor, the needy, the outcast, the vulnerable, the orphan. He breaks into hopeless situations, reaches out, and lifts up the hurting. He removes and rescues them from the dirt and poverty, from the situations where they are discarded, ignored, and mistreated. Then He carefully and gently sets them down with people, His people, who will care for them, esteem them, appreciate them, and value them. That's what God has done for Amahle and for so many other children at Acres of Love.

# Twenty

## GATSHA

• • •

At a very young age, Gatsha suffered a terrible head injury. He became a paraplegic and was later diagnosed with spinal tuberculosis. Because of his disability, his family treated him poorly and eventually abandoned him. He was found under a pile of old clothes locked in a closet.

Gatsha came to Acres of Love at the age of fourteen. He underwent several surgeries to address his medical needs and was in a wheelchair. Everyone who met him couldn't believe how amazing he was. A dedicated brother, he was soft spoken, kind, and an advocate for other children with disabilities. Gerda worked tirelessly to get him into a good school because he was incredibly smart. At first they didn't want to let him in, but she was persistent and they eventually accepted him. He went on to university, studied to be an accountant, and had an internship at a prestigious production company.

But then at the age of twenty-two, Gatsha suddenly passed away. Everyone at Acres of Love was devastated. When our Forever Families gathered to celebrate his life and mourn him, the teenagers and young adults stepped into a leadership role. They hosted the event, shared heartfelt stories and memories of their treasured brother and friend, and spoke of the tremendous impact he made on everyone.

Gerda recently shared with me a text she'd sent Gatsha just before his death:

*Gatsha, I just want to say that everyone who meets you has such an amazing report about you. Your kindness and manners are outstanding. So proud of who you are. You will go very far in life. He has a wonderful plan for you. Love, Mom Gerda*

He texted back:

*This means a lot to me. I appreciate the recognition and I hope to stay humble as I am. It is just the work of God and I am glad that He lives inside of me and that He is displayed by the type of person I am. Thank you very much and I love you too.*

# Twenty-One

## LIYANA

...

One day Acres of Love received a call for a new admission: a little girl named Liyana, who was ten years old. She and her little sister went to buy milk one day, and when they returned, their mother, who had been sick with AIDS, was lying dead in their tiny shack. Liyana struggled to take care of her little sister, and they were placed in foster care with a woman living in a squatter camp.

Staff members were told that Liyana had a disease in her colon. Gerda researched the disease and quickly became overwhelmed because the condition looked so demanding. Liyana's gut had become incapacitated, and she had no control over her bowels. Her foster mom mistreated her terribly because of her condition and would make her stay out in the freezing cold and wash the clothes and blankets she soiled.

Acres of Love had just opened a new Forever Home that had six little boys living in it. Gerda decided to bring Liyana and her sister into that home because the boys were all so little that they wouldn't tease Liyana for having accidents. She could have her own room, and the staff would be able to find out what was really going on.

When she arrived, Liyana could sit only in a leaning-back position. Her abdomen was hard and extended, and she looked like she was eight months pregnant. They immediately took her to a gastro specialist, and the doctor didn't know how she was even alive. Her lower intestines were so filled with waste that it was pressing into her lungs, making breathing difficult. She needed to go to the hospital immediately.

Over the next two years, Liyana endured multiple surgeries. Eventually they put in a colostomy bag, which gave her instant relief. As she was feeling better, she began opening up to our staff. She told the story of her abuse in detail, how they would send her to a rural hospital and not really do any investigation or anything to help her. Children were lying all around her, and they would just die.

As staff members addressed Liyana's medical needs, they also began to research the best possible education path for her because she had missed much schooling trying to care for her little sister. They ended up finding a great school that met her individual needs, and she was able to graduate from secondary school. She chose a trade in the baking industry and today has an excellent job at a lovely coffee shop, where she makes stunning cakes.

## · WHAT IF? ·

The day the doctor was examining Liyana and making plans for her first surgery, a man walked into our U.S. office in Southern California. He said, "I'm not a good man. Use this money however you see fit." He wrote a check for $20,000 and walked out. The cost of Liyana's treatment came out to be the exact amount of that donation.

Time and time again, we see God's hand in every single detail of this work. When He gives us an assignment, we get to respond immediately in obedience. He doesn't want us to worry about how it will all work out and delay because we don't have the answers up front. He just wants us to trust Him and get in motion. His provision is always wrapped up in the assignment. He will provide everything we need to execute the task at hand; all we have to do is be willing and available.

Caring for orphans is what God does. Liyana is His child, and He loves her, has plans for her, and will provide for her. When He brought her to Acres of Love, the staff said yes to her—to her needs, to the medical treatment, and to whatever else was necessary. Ryan and Gerda trusted God to provide for every one of her needs, even though they couldn't see at the time how it was all going to work out.

# Twenty-Two

## MPISO

• • •

Gerda works well with the Acres of Love team, even though she lives in the U.S. and they are in South Africa. She realizes she can't make a unilateral decision from the other side of the world about which children to take in. The team in South Africa is in the trenches doing the hard work, and all of them work together to make decisions about the children they rescue.

When they received a call about Mpiso, a child with cerebral palsy, the team resisted. The doctors who work closely with Acres of Love warned the team that they weren't equipped for a child like this and advised them not to take him. The team emailed Gerda and told her they didn't feel they were ready to take Mpiso in because, at that point in time, they had never dealt with a child with his types of needs.

Gerda didn't argue. She just said, "I know what type of care we can provide that child. Whether we are equipped or not, we would give that child unconditional love. We know we have the resources to provide good care even if we have to learn a few things along the way.

Why don't you go and find another organization that will match what we can do for him and then let me know?"

So the team phoned around and looked at some places. They returned to Gerda in humility and reported that there was no other place that could provide the level of care they could. Gerda replied, "Well, there you are. We are going to bring him in!" Even though the team didn't have the experience or expertise to care for a child with cerebral palsy, Gerda was confident that God would provide all that Mpiso needed through their unconditional love.

Gerda had a special reason for being interested in Mpiso. A short time earlier, a man she'd never met walked up to her after a church service and said, "I have a word from the Lord for you. You are the one that God is going to send the children that no one wants. Just help them. Just do it." That encouraging word gave her the spiritual courage to say yes to more of these difficult special needs cases. God had prepared her, and she knew she could trust Him.

She told me, "When you make that step of obedience, the Lord supernaturally provides. He provides the resources, the money, etc.— but He also provided the confidence of the team. When the team makes progress, they get more and more confidence. They get the joy of serving these kids. Now when special needs kids arrive, everyone starts rejoicing because there is a whole different level of anointing and blessing on Acres of Love."

At the same time Acres of Love admitted Mpiso, a twenty-year-old girl began volunteering at the home where he was living. She saw him and said, "Oh, my goodness—look at this soccer player!" She worked in a school with cerebral palsy kids, and she fell in love with Mpiso and started working with him. She told the staff that if they could find a facilitator for the school, she would pick Mpiso up every day so he could go to the school where she worked. She began inviting him to go to youth group with her every Friday night at her church, and they spent more and more time together. A beautiful bond formed between them. She remained committed to him, year in and year out. When she eventually married, she chose a man who also adored Mpiso. They adopted him and ended up moving to London.

## • WHAT IF? •

What if that stranger hadn't walked up to Gerda and shared with her what the Lord was telling him? What if Gerda hadn't believed what he said or allowed it to impact her work with the kids at Acres of Love? What if she had agreed with the doctors and her staff and declined to take in Mpiso because of his special needs? He never would have met his adoptive mother, who was a perfect match to care for him long term.

Gerda's belief in God and her subsequent obedience provided Mpiso with a life he never would have known. And because of the way God showed up in all these details, she and her team felt more confident about taking in children with more extensive needs. God created each of those children; He knows their needs, and He has a plan for their lives that is good. He constantly and tirelessly works in the lives of His people, and when we follow His lead, He shows up and we get to see Him.

# Twenty-Three

## ISISI AND DUMISANI

...

One day Gerda received an email from a boy who had been adopted out of Acres of Love as a young child. "Hi, my name is Dumisani and I was one of your first babies," he wrote. "I want to say thank you for my God-given life."

Dumisani was one of the first six babies to come to Acres of Love. During those early days, a man and woman who used to volunteer regularly at Acres of Love fell in love with him. Whenever a child knows somebody who visited has taken an interest in them, a change comes over that child. Dumisani used to stand at the window and look up the driveway, waiting for the volunteers who would come at five to help bathe and feed him, play in the garden, and take him for walks. Dumisani wouldn't eat with everyone else; he would stand there and wait for his "mom and dad" to come feed him. After just a few months, they decided to adopt him, and Gerda hadn't heard from him until she received his email.

Gerda wrote back to him, "Dumisani, I remember you! You came from the hospital with us on that first day. You came with Isisi, a girl who is still with us. You sat on my son Darren's lap in the car on the way from the hospital."

Gerda sent photos of him and Isisi taken right after they'd come to Acres of Love; they were sitting together in a little red sand pit in the backyard. She also included a recent picture of Isisi. Gerda learned that Dumisani was a wonderful young man who attended a private Christian school right by Isisi's house. Two of Isisi's Acres of Love sisters also attended Dumisani's school.

He came with his mom and dad to reunite with Isisi since they had such a special history together. Dumisani's family embraced her. They started inviting her to youth group and over to their house for dinner, and Dumisani and Isisi became very close friends. They spent more and more time together, and eventually he asked her to be his date to his senior prom. In preparation for this special night, Gerda brought Isisi a stunning, long red dress from America to wear to the dance. She looked like a princess, and the pictures of them together the night of the dance are lovely.

Isisi told Gerda that Dumisani is amazing, and she hopes one day she will marry somebody like him.

# Twenty-four

## PHILANO

• • •

The teenage daughter of a very successful banker in Johannesburg came to Acres of Love to volunteer with the children. When the banker heard about this, he became concerned about his daughter working with what he called "AIDS orphans." He insisted on going with them so he could supervise while his daughter volunteered.

One of the Acres of Love staff saw the banker standing around and assumed he was also there to volunteer. So she handed him one of the little boys, an infant named Philano. The banker sat there in his fancy suit and held one of the "AIDS orphans" on his lap. Week after week, the banker returned to Acres of Love with his daughter. Before long, the bond between him and Philano began to grow, and the banker starting going to Acres of Love on his own just to see Philano. He would go in the middle of the day to greet him when Philano was coming home from an appointment, or he'd wait for him to wake up from a nap so he could play with him and feed him his lunch. As Philano grew into a toddler, the banker started taking him fishing and on other fun outings. The banker eventually became a member of the Acres of Love board and an influential fundraiser for the organization.

When Philano was eventually diagnosed with fetal alcohol syndrome, the banker focused his attention on research and looking for answers to help Acres of Love help Philano. Finally he said, "Throw all the books out. We are going to adopt him!"

Acres of Love has an amazing impact on people. I've heard many stories of volunteers becoming full-time staff members, of reluctant and fearful adults falling in love and adopting, and of staff members staying on board for *several* years because of the commitment they feel for the children and the organization's vision. It doesn't take long to realize there is just something divine about Acres of Love. It's special, shockingly successful, and setting the standard for orphan care. As you get up close to it, you are drawn in deeper, and the more engaged you become, the more convinced you are that it is supernaturally blessed. This is God's heart—caring for orphans. Ryan and Gerda put their work in God's hands and trusted Him with every aspect of it, and in response, He is multiplying their efforts and providing everything and every person needed to get the job done.

Most of the time, people get involved with Acres of Love thinking that they can help in some way, be a blessing. That's what happened with me. But I quickly realized that the blessing is all mine because I am up close and personal with the very hand of God.

# Twenty-five

## THABISA

...

Some of our youngest girls have fallen victim to the myth that still plays out sometimes in South Africa—that sex with a virgin will cure a person with HIV/AIDS. Thabisa was raped before she was even one year old. When she was two years old, she was abandoned in a hospital, and two years later, Acres of Love finally learned of her.

When she came to Acres of Love, the staff discovered that she was deaf and needed to have reconstructive surgery to repair the physical damage caused by her abuse. In her first year with them, she went to 130 doctors' appointments, was diagnosed with HIV, and suffered from a terrible lung condition. Her hollow eyes and withdrawn demeanor showed deep pain. Staff members worked diligently to provide her with therapeutic sessions to address her social and emotional well-being, and they enrolled her in an excellent school for the deaf. Her house mom and the other children in her Forever Home went every Saturday to learn sign language with her. Before this, Thabisa couldn't communicate with anyone; she was trapped. But now, though she is still reserved, she loves to play with her sisters, harvest vegetables from the garden, and attend school. Most important, she has found her smile and her confidence.

Recently at one of our Forever Home dedications, her sisters wanted to perform a worship song for everyone. As the others sang with their voices, Thabisa sang with her hands.

## • WHAT IF? •

These are just a few stories that represent the difference that Acres of Love is making in the lives of orphaned children in South Africa. Every child who comes in has a heartbreaking story; they've experienced massive loss and endured pain, suffering, and trauma. Every child brings with them a past that could dictate their future and perpetuate the curse of poverty—*but God.* He has intervened in the lives of these children. He has rescued them and is restoring them. Now their futures are bright and the possibilities are endless. The young adults who have "launched" from Acres of Love are healthy, thriving, educated, faith-filled, capable members of society. Those who have varying degrees of special needs that require our long-term care are welcomed to stay with us forever.

What if Ryan and Gerda hadn't said yes when God called them to start just with that first home? What if they were too distracted, too scared, and too riddled with feelings of inadequacy? What would have become of the hundreds of children who beat the odds as the rest of us watched in awe? What if the staff members and donors hadn't been given the opportunity to experience God in this way? What if I hadn't been able to learn from Ryan, Gerda, and these amazing children? Ryan and Gerda's "yes" has made an impact that goes on forever and ever. It's too big to measure or quantify.

What if God is calling you to something that could have massive implications? You could say no because of fear or distraction.

But what if you said yes?

# Part Four

## THE SEARCH FOR MORE OF GOD

· · ·

# Twenty-Six

## THE DISCOVERY
## OF MORE

...

In May 2015, I was asked to share my testimony with MOPS (Mothers of Preschoolers) at a local church. Afterward, a woman named Megan came up to talk to me. She was crying and trembling, and she explained that she'd been praying for something to be involved with. Overwhelmed with everything I had shared about Acres of Love, she wanted to learn more. I suggested she host a dinner party at her house and invite some friends. I would do a presentation about Acres of Love and invite them to get involved with the organization.

She enthusiastically sent out the invitations that afternoon and hosted the dinner party the following Friday evening. Initially she received a great response and expected a good turnout, but in the end, only one couple and her dad showed up. I could tell she was disappointed and a little embarrassed.

"It's all right," I reassured her. I wasn't concerned with how many people came. I had faith that God was in the details of the event and that He'd brought the exact people who were supposed to be there.

That evening, I shared about Acres of Love and answered the usual questions. While the other couple never did get involved, Megan and her husband were moved to compassion, very touched by the work we were doing. They have become some of our most committed and invested donor partners, as well as our dear friends.

But something else also happened that night. I met Blaine Cook, Megan's dad. He had just returned from Brazil, where he often travels on ministry trips. He nonchalantly mentioned that he'd witnessed several amazing miracles while he was there. Intrigued, I bombarded the poor guy with questions. He told me about a crippled, deformed hand being healed and a missing nose growing back on a woman's face right in front of him.

I couldn't believe what I was hearing and asked again and again, "Are you serious? Come on! Really?"

He assured me he was telling the truth and that these kinds of things happen all the time when he goes on these trips. I sat next to him at dinner and listened as he told me story after story of miracles and healings he had seen and even been a part of. He also shared with me his testimony of being baptized in the Holy Spirit, something I'd never even heard about before. Twenty years ago, he'd apprehensively gone to a prayer meeting with his wife, and the Lord touched him in a powerful way. He wept for months as God healed his heart and transformed him.

As I listened to Blaine that night, I learned that God was so much bigger than I knew. There was *more* of Him—more for me. Blaine introduced me to a whole new realm with the Lord that I never knew was possible, and something ignited inside me that changed the course and direction of my walk with Him.

Because of the work I was doing in South Africa, Blaine told me about his friend, Heidi Baker, who was from Laguna Beach, California, but served as a full-time missionary in Mozambique. He gave me a documentary about her and told me to watch it.

A couple of days later, I invited Sue and Gretchen to watch the movie with me. We popped in the DVD, pushed play, and none of us were ever the same again. Here was this tiny blonde lady born and raised just a few miles away from where I live. She was a powerhouse, filled to overflowing with love, power, and authority as God used her to do miraculous things in Mozambique. She practically glowed as she did things I never, ever thought possible. She had given up her comfortable Southern California life to live in the dirt in Africa. In addition to adopting countless children, she fed thousands of people every single day, ran a school for missionaries, traveled the world to preach and minister, delivered witch doctors of demons, healed the deaf and blind, and even raised people from the dead. This was radical stuff.

We couldn't believe our eyes. How was it that all these things were happening, and no one knew about it? Why wasn't this all over the news? What did Heidi have that others didn't? Whatever it was, I wanted it! I wanted the intimate, life-giving relationship I could see she had with the Lord. My heart began to long for the kind of faith she possessed, and I wanted to make the same impact in the world that she was making.

Something in me came awake. Now that I had seen what was possible with God, I was determined to go after it for myself. I was hungrier than ever for the things of the Spirit. Feverishly I began reading, studying, praying, seeking, and searching. The more I learned, the more I realized I didn't know and the more I wanted to learn. My appetite for the Word and the Holy Spirit became insatiable.

The next week Blaine invited me to attend a regular prayer meeting he has in his home. He let me come early so I could sit down with him alone and talk about all the things I was learning.

He shared with me about the Holy Spirit and the gifts of the Spirit, and then he looked at me and said, "Kim, you have the gift of healing. I can see it all over you."

I stared at him in surprise. *What?* What did that mean, and what in the world was I supposed to do with it?

The meeting started as the house filled with people. A couple of guys led worship for about an hour, and I loved it. It was beautiful. People were engaged and singing, some with their hands raised, some kneeling, some dancing. They worshipped God freely, lost in the moment and comfortable expressing themselves. It seemed like such a safe and accepting environment. People were at peace, not worried about what they looked like but completely focused on their time worshipping God, on experiencing Him.

Blaine briefly spoke and then invited people to share what they were hearing from God. They encouraged one another, prayed for each other, and blessed and commissioned people going to places all over the world. Some prophesied and some gave words of knowledge; many spoke in tongues. For me, the gathering was a real example of what "church" should look like: believers coming together and sharing their gifts of the Spirit to exhort and build each other up to do the work of the ministry. The whole experience was very new to me and unlike any other gathering of believers I had ever been a part of. I was a little hesitant, but I was also intrigued and—more important—felt at peace.

Later, I got my hands on several of Heidi Baker's books and just consumed them. She spoke of the Holy Spirit the same way Blaine did. Seeing how full of faith, passionate, and surrendered she was, I was inspired by her "all in" lifestyle and admired how she had given up a normal life to live among and care for the poorest people in the world.

While I thought she was quite radical, and unlike any other Christian I had ever heard of, I felt like I could relate to her. I had long desired to give more of myself to Christ and to live a life of service, so I could appreciate her hunger and understand her devotion. She was real, and she challenged and inspired me. In fact, most of the things she so eloquently said in her books were things I had already thought about, prayed about, and talked with God over, so she confirmed them within me—things I had asked God to confirm.

I felt like He had divinely led me to Blaine and Heidi to further show me what it looked like to truly believe Him and act like it. In addition to my close friends Ryan and Gerda, these were people who really took their faith seriously. They were living it out and surrendering their personal agendas to serve God wholeheartedly.

## • WHAT IF? •

I began to notice a rising boldness within me to tell people what I was learning and experiencing with God. I wanted them to know there was more available in relationship with Him. I had been walking closely with the Lord for ten years but was just now learning about the things of the Spirit—why was that? Why weren't all believers in Jesus doing the things Blaine and Heidi were doing? I began to ask myself some very important questions:

What if God wanted to use *me* to heal people?

What if I could go deeper with Him and experience intimacy with Him the way Heidi talked about? What if I could hear His voice like she did?

A fire lit within me to learn and explore and then share and teach. If the "more" of God was out there, I didn't want anyone to miss it, myself included. So I set out to discover what would happen if I believed God for more.

Heidi's words have stayed with me:

*Yes, God wants you to do signs and wonders. But the love of God manifested through you is what people really need. So you must first see His face. You must become so close to His very heartbeat that you can feel what others feel. I want to live as if I am hidden in His very heart, where His thoughts become my thoughts and His ways become my ways. This is how we will reach the world.*[4]

---

4 Heidi Baker, *Compelled by Love: How to Change the World Through the Simple Power of Love in Action* (Lake Mary, FL: Charisma House, 2013).

# Twenty-Seven

## GOING AFTER GOD

...

When I found out Heidi Baker was going to be speaking in Oklahoma, I jumped on a plane with Sue and Gretchen. Filled with anticipation, I was convinced that something amazing was going to happen—I would be rocked by God and never be the same. I couldn't wait!

At the meeting, everyone around me was dancing, singing spontaneously, falling on the ground, weeping, shaking, or speaking in tongues. They were obviously in some awesome "God zone" and being touched by the Holy Spirit, and I wanted in on the action. I wanted to have a powerful encounter with God and be so overtaken by the Holy Spirit that everything else fell away. I begged God over and over to show Himself to me.

"Please, Lord," I prayed. "Show Yourself to me. Reveal Yourself. I want to see You and know You. Take all of me. Do something."

But I felt nothing.

A man was walking around laying his hands on people's heads. He prayed for them and asked God to fill them with the Holy Spirit. Everyone he touched had an obvious encounter with God. As he made his way closer to me, I knew this was it—this was my moment.

The man came up to me, put his hands on my head, and shouted something. I leaned back and fell onto the floor. I lay there for a couple of minutes, feeling nothing and thinking to myself, *Maybe something happens after you fall down on the ground. I'll wait. Lord? I don't feel anything. Nope, nothing. I feel nothing.* The bottom of some lady's skirt kept brushing my face, and I stood back up, feeling ridiculous.

I looked around at all the people who were clearly caught up in something I was not experiencing. Heidi was up on the stage, praying on her knees, and people were all around her. I thought to myself, *I've come a long way from home to get something from God. I will not leave here without it!* I actually crawled up the stairs to the stage to get closer to her. When I reached my hand out toward her, she put her hand on top of mine and left it there for a long time while she prayed. I quietly begged the Lord, "Yes—now. Please, give me something. Please!"

But again, nothing happened. Disappointed and a little embarrassed, I wondered, *Why not me?* What was I doing wrong? Why were all these other people getting something from God that He wasn't giving me? Maybe I was wrong to want more. Maybe there *wasn't* more.

I went home feeling disappointed and sort of dejected. I didn't understand what was happening to all those other people and felt hurt that God wasn't doing something for me. I spent a lot of time praying about it. Was I acting too desperate? Was I trying to make something happen?

Finally, I felt the Lord tenderly tell me, "The truth is, you *are* desperate. You *are* trying to make something happen. But it's because you want more. I love that."

During this conversation with God, I thought of the Bible story about the bleeding woman. She had been bleeding for twelve years and had suffered a great deal from several doctors. When she heard about Jesus, she pushed through a crowd to get close to Him, so she could touch the hem of His robe. Desperate, she knew that if she could just touch His clothes, she would be healed—and she was.

"It is your faith that has made you well," Jesus told her.

I've always appreciated this woman's persistence and desperation. That was what I was feeling. I didn't want just to hear about other people's experiences or watch them unfold right in front of me. I didn't want just to read the Bible and gain "head knowledge" about God—I wanted to encounter Him and be close to Him. I wanted to feel Him and know His power. I wanted to be caught up in the Spirit. And I knew God was telling me that He was pleased with my desire.

I continued to study the baptism of the Holy Spirit, signs and wonders, healings, miracles, and prophecy (which, I learned, is personal revelation from the Holy Spirit about someone in order to edify and encourage them). I would get up early every morning, around 4:30, to pray, read, study, and spend quiet time with the Lord before the rest of my family woke up. My desire for God led me to start blogging regularly and posting thoughts and Scriptures on social media about my faith and all the things I was learning.

It had taken years for me to get to this place, and I found I wanted to encourage other people to take their own journeys into the more of God.

# Twenty-Eight

## THREE-BRAIDED CORD

...

When I first started following the Lord, I struggled with my friendships. I'd lived thirty years of my life as an unbeliever, so I was surrounded by people who weren't walking with the Lord either. As God began to strengthen my faith and change my heart, my priorities and desires changed. Without making a conscious decision to change my lifestyle, I gradually noticed I no longer watched certain TV shows, had a desire to gossip, or wanted to spend my time at bars drinking. Nor was I consumed with climbing the social status ladder in my community.

As I began to feel lonely because no one around me shared my passions, I asked God to bring godly friends into my life and surround me with people who had the same beliefs and priorities. I wanted friends who would love to study the Bible with me, go to Christian concerts, and talk about Jesus over a nice glass of red wine.

After a time, He answered that prayer by bringing me Sue and Gretchen. They loved the Lord, were committed to following Him, and shared my desire to serve with Acres of Love. We spent hours talking about Jesus, Scripture, leading our families in the things of faith, and honoring God in our marriages. These women were down to earth and smart, loving and generous. I knew God had put us together on purpose; it was a divine, supernatural sisterhood. We started calling ourselves the "Three-Braided Cord," like Ecclesiastes 4:12 talks about: "A person standing alone can be attacked and defeated, but two can stand back-to-back and conquer. Three are even better, for a triple-braided cord is not easily broken."

In November 2015, Sue and Gretchen joined me on another trip to South Africa so I could do some research for this book, interview kids and staff at Acres of Love, and visit key places. While in South Africa, we were able to celebrate the ten-year anniversary of our Bridges Forever Home. We invited all the kids to join us for lunch at the Acres of Love Provision Home, which houses all our staff offices. It is a beautiful estate decorated elegantly with African décor, and there are pictures all over the house of the Acres of Love kids. The home is inviting and a place where the kids love to gather for birthday parties, holidays, and retreats, as well as to visit with donor partners from all over the world.

We got up early that morning and helped Gerda get everything ready for the lunch. She drove us to a flower mart to handpick beautiful, exotic flowers so we would have a big bouquet for the table. Then we drove to the best bakery in town, where she picked out delicious-smelling rolls for the sandwiches. She also took us to the best butcher to get their famous sausages. We were moved by the lengths she went to so this party would be special for the kids. Only the best places for her beloved children.

When I commented on how she did things for the children with such excellence, she replied, "Love is in the details. Wouldn't we bring Jesus our best gift?"

The lunch was wonderful. I prayed over the kids and expressed our love and support. We played games, spun cotton candy, told stories, and rejoiced in God's blessings.

On this trip, Sue, Gretchen, and I had planned to visit the hospital where Ryan and Gerda picked up the first six babies to come to Acres of Love. We wanted to understand what the situation was like for orphans and abandoned babies before they were rescued. How were they treated in a hospital setting? We hoped to gain experiential knowledge of what they had been through and the type of rural communities they came from.

Gerda arranged for Peter, one of the Acres of Love drivers, to take us to the hospital. It was a long drive from Johannesburg, out through wide-open plains and past many poor areas. Peter is a tall, dark African man in his forties who always wears a nicely pressed Acres of Love collared shirt. He has the warmest, most infectious smile and greets people with a loving embrace. He's a husband and father but lives away from his family to work at Acres of Love and sends the money home to them. He drives the kids around all day, all around Johannesburg. He starts his "runs" early in the morning and takes the kids from their various Forever Homes to school, to therapy and doctors' appointments, to tutoring, to practice, to church, and back again.

"What do you like most about your job?" we asked.

He proudly boasted of his "VIPs." These are the special needs children at Acres of Love. Some are in wheelchairs or have major debilitating health issues; some have developmental delays.

"I really love to be with them," he said. He sees them every day and knows what they like and what they don't, how to hold them just the right way or what they are trying to say with their grunts and groans. He can tell when they aren't feeling well and worries about them when he's not with them.

It was a precious thing to hear him talk about those kids. It was just another reminder of how blessed Acres of Love is. The people who work for the organization are not just employees; it's not just a job to them. The people God has brought to the organization love the Lord, feel called to this work, and consider themselves blessed to be a part of it. It's a divine and supernatural undertaking.

As we neared the hospital, Peter told us, "We'll only be able to drive by the hospital because it's an unsafe area. Security won't just let us go in and look around."

I was disappointed because I really wanted to walk the halls, look at the children, smell the smells, and hear the sounds. I felt it was important to understand the types of conditions our first children were rescued out of.

"Please, God," I prayed. "Make a way for us."

When we reached the hospital, I asked Peter to pull up to the security gate and just *see* if we could drive into the parking lot. He spoke to the man at the gate in a tribal language. The man searched our car and then motioned for us to pull forward into the lot. We parked and nervously approached several intimidating security guards at the hospital entrance. Peter again spoke in a language we didn't recognize. The guards looked us up and down and never once smiled or responded with a friendly gesture, but they allowed us to follow them inside.

We walked down a long, dark hallway to an office where a large woman, the hospital supervisor, was reading a newspaper. She looked inconvenienced and annoyed as she jerked her hand, gesturing for us to sit down.

"What do you want?" she asked, looking at me.

I told her that we were with Acres of Love. Fifteen years ago, we had taken six children from their hospital, and we wished to see the place where our first babies had come from.

She picked up the phone and called her managing supervisor. After speaking in the same tribal language, she hung up and signaled for us to follow her. She started walking us around the hospital and telling us all about the place. We couldn't believe it. Walking behind her, we tried to keep our excited giggles to ourselves and thanked God for opening doors for us. The woman relaxed and let her guard down with us; informative and thorough, she ushered us through every inch of that hospital and even invited us to come back again another time.

As we made our way to the children's ward, we walked by a litter of stray kittens that clearly lived there inside the hospital. It was strange to us to see kittens in a hospital, but it was strange only to us. No one else seemed surprised by their presence.

We entered a section of the hospital where the supervisor allowed us to visit with some of the patients. It was a large, dimly lit room with about twenty cribs, all of them filled. Most of the cribs had no sheets and no blankets, and many of the babies were crying alone, without anyone attending them.

I was drawn to one tiny baby girl who was screaming in an incubator. The alarms on the machines above her were going off, indicating that her oxygen levels were dangerously low. I could see that she had a nasal cannula to supply oxygen, but it had fallen out of her nose.

"Can I help the baby?" I asked an unconcerned nurse who was sitting behind her desk.

The nurse nodded, so I leaned forward to replace the cannula and then carefully lifted the baby into my arms. She was burning hot with a fever; her diaper was warm and heavy and smelled of horrible diarrhea. Trying to comfort her, I rocked her small body and fought back tears.

I looked over into the corner and saw a toddler crying on a bare mattress; she looked to have cerebral palsy and she was all alone. No one tended to her. Looking another direction, I saw a little girl with a massively deformed head. It was completely sunken in on one side. Her eyes bulged out of her face, and her arms stuck straight out from her body. Her young mother was there holding her; the woman looked confused, exhausted, and overwhelmed.

On our ride home, we barely said a word to one another. Everything inside me felt like it was weeping. My heart broke into a million pieces for those children. I couldn't stand that their care wasn't like the kind my own children would receive if they were in a hospital in California, and I hated that most of the children were there alone, without a parent sitting next to their crib and advocating for them. Another part of me was furious because I wanted to do something to help, something to alleviate their pain and bring them hope, but I felt helpless and crushed.

When we returned to our hotel room, I sobbed into my pillow, leaving it riddled with mascara stains. I kept saying, "I just don't understand!" I was confused about a God who would allow innocent children to suffer like that. How was this fair? These children were paying a price for something they didn't do. None of them deserved that kind of life, with so much pain and loss. Guilt overwhelmed me when I thought about the blessed life I lived back in the States.

I wanted to do something to help these kids—I wanted to save them. More than ever, I committed myself to work hard on behalf of Acres of Love, so we could rescue more children.

# Twenty-Nine

## GOD OF THE POOR

...

The next morning, we left to meet the kids from the Bridges Forever Home at their church in Boksburg.

Some of our favorite memories from this trip to South Africa involved conversations with the various drivers who would take us from place to place. We loved to ask questions about where they lived, where they were from, what their lives were like.

This particular Uber driver told us he was from Zimbabwe and, like many others, had fled his country to come to South Africa to find work so he could help take care of his family. "The journey to South Africa was long and dangerous," he said. He swam through crocodile-infested waters to get here, and many of the people he was traveling with were killed by the crocodiles or by lions, or they were trapped in the large shipping containers they were hiding in and left to die. His son was mugged for his cell phone and killed.

As we listened to his story, we were stunned. This man had been through so much; he had witnessed horrific things and experienced heartache. Born and raised in the United States, we had difficulty understanding the extremes people chose to go through just to live in a place where there was more opportunity to provide for themselves and their families.

Later when the three of us talked about this driver, we realized God was igniting compassion in us for people who lived in poverty and were desperate to improve the quality of their lives. This compassion wasn't just so we could be more grateful about our own situations, but it also reminded us that we are blessed so we can be a blessing to others. The Bible teaches that when someone has been given much, much will be required in return (Luke 12:48). Everything we have comes from the Lord and is a gift from Him. The money in our wallets, the jobs we have, the skills we possess, the very breath in our lungs—it's all from Him. We don't belong to ourselves but to God, who bought us at a very high price (1 Cor. 6:20). Instead of living with our heads in the sand, we can be aware of the needs of the people around us and step out of our comfort zones to help meet those needs.

A couple of days after meeting the driver from Zimbabwe, my friends and I sat down with Gerda for lunch at a beautiful winery called Rust en Vrede in Cape Town. We shared with her that as we looked at all the suffering, poverty, and pain around us, we felt like there was nothing we could do to make a bit of difference, not when the whole country had so much need. We'd spent countless hours talking about it, dissecting it, questioning what our role was in the midst of this pain and heartache, and praying that God would give us wisdom and use us to alleviate the pain of the people in this country we loved so much. Our hearts were heavy, and we were growing more and more tired.

Gerda diagnosed us with "paralysis of analysis," and we realized she was right. We were overanalyzing the problem and feeling like it was too much to bear, which left us paralyzed and unable to do anything.

"The accident has happened," she said. "The car has already crashed and there are victims everywhere. Get into problem-solving mode." She reminded us that the enemy comes to steal, kill, and destroy (John 10:10). We needed to ask the Lord to bring us back to focus. We're vessels for God, to be used by Him as He pleases. Instead of being overwhelmed at the size of the problem, it's important just to sit with people in their pain, really see them, validate them, touch them, give them hope in Jesus, and usher in the Holy Spirit to everyone, everywhere, in every situation.

Gerda said, "When you turn on a faucet, the tap doesn't bring the water. It's just a conduit." Our role is to be that conduit for people, so they can experience the love of God.

One morning a few days after visiting with Gerda at the vineyard, we had the privilege of hosting a lovely breakfast for the Acres of Love house moms in the Cape Town region. We listened as these wise, committed women shared stories of their young charges. These are some of the sickest kids, those with the greatest medical needs. Anyone caring for them would be overwhelmed and exhausted, but these house moms spoke about their kids with so much love, concern, and pride. This clearly isn't just a job for them, something they do to pay the bills; these women aren't just going through the motions. They truly do see these children as their own.

One of the moms told us she is "working for her heavenly crown." They see their role as house moms as a calling, a way of serving the Lord. They care for their children with excellence because of their love for God; it's His love that flows through them and empowers them to love the kids with a divine love. These women know God in a way many people do not. They said yes to Him and are obediently living their lives, day in and day out, in response to Him.

We began to see a distinct pattern with everyone involved with Acres of Love. From Ryan and Gerda to the house parents, to the social workers, drivers, assistants, teachers, volunteers, and donors—every person involved knows God deeply. He called them into this work, and they are doing it for Him. The people are anointed and the ministry is blessed.

Honestly, it seems to me that everyone who comes into contact with Acres of Love is transformed. It's not just about providing a bowl of food and a blanket for orphans; it's about love and healing and bringing your very best gift to the Father. Because Ryan and Gerda said yes to the Lord fifteen years ago, *thousands* of people all over the world are being impacted. It's like a pebble thrown into a pond, and the ripples just go on and on forever. There is no way to measure the eternal consequences this work is having. Ryan and Gerda couldn't have known how big this would get, how far it would reach, how blessed it would be. They were just available, willing, and obedient. They believed God and got in motion, stepping out in faith, and now look at what God had done with their yes. He was using their lives to touch, heal, and transform people all over the world.

Shortly before leaving South Africa, we randomly connected with a woman named Karin who lived near Stellenbosch, Cape Town, in a township called Kayamandi. Founded in the early 1950s as part of the increased segregation during the apartheid regime, the area was originally built to house exclusively black migrant male laborers employed on the farms in the Stellenbosch area.

Karin invited us to her home for the weekly "reconciliation luncheon" that she'd been hosting for years. She was a retired social worker, and her husband and their three young children had been involved with the township of Kayamandi for many years. At the very beginning of their ministry, they volunteered with their church to go into the township and run special programs for the impoverished community. But then they felt the Lord telling them that instead of going in and out of the community to help, He wanted them to really "love their neighbor" by becoming one with them . . . literally. So they moved into the township and lived among its people. They were the only white people in a town of approximately thirty thousand blacks.

"It was a hard transition at first, for our family and for the community," she told us. But after a time, the people accepted them and really began to respect them.

Karin began to host these weekly luncheons because she wanted to bring the people together in a safe environment—people who wouldn't normally spend time with one another. She found that many from different tribes held long-standing grudges against each other. So she invited anyone who wanted to come, cooked a beautiful lunch, set a huge table, served food on lovely plates, and used her own silver and crystal. After sharing a short devotional, she would pray and invite everyone to answer an interesting question she posed while they enjoyed lunch.

The day we joined them, she spread us out among her guests. The food was delicious, and we got to know one another as we all took turns sharing a childhood memory. We found the people warm and welcoming; their different stories and perspectives were fascinating, and we were moved by Karin's ability to love these people and bring them together in peace. Again we were in awe of God, who had unexpectedly and divinely introduced us to Karin and allowed us to see another example of a person really living out their faith, day after day, with surrender and trust.

In the short couple of hours we spent at Karin's house, we learned life-long lessons about bravery, risk, obedience, and genuine love for God's people. From Karin I learned all over again that God wants us to love our neighbors, whoever they are and wherever they come from. Our neighbors are not just those who look, act, and live like we do. Sometimes our "neighbor" might live in our house or on our street. Sometimes a neighbor might live in the bad part of town or even on the other side of the world. There are times when loving a neighbor is radical and risky; it might even be dangerous. But if we genuinely want to follow God, we need to do what He tells us.

The day we left South Africa to fly home, I spoke to a crowd of five thousand people at an Herbalife conference, a company that has been a financial partner of ours for years, helping provide healthy foods to keep our kids thriving and strong. I thanked the company for their continued commitment and shared with them success stories of some of our kids who were once very ill but now were whole and healthy.

Without planning to, I found myself continually mentioning God, sharing how we put our faith in Him for the children's healing and restoration. I even told the story of Ayanda, the little girl who was miraculously healed of cancer. The crowd cheered and gave me a standing ovation when I finished speaking. It was an anointed morning, and I was thrilled I had been genuine and bold about our reliance on God. It was an incredible feeling to stand up in front of an audience that size and testify to the work of the Lord.

## · WHAT IF? ·

After we returned home, my two friends and I spent time together and realized all three of us felt the same way: We were drawn to know God more than ever, and we wanted other people to experience Him the same way we had on the other side of the world. Why was He easy to recognize in Africa but hard to find at home in Southern California? Why was God working so much in other parts of the world? He was performing incredible miracles in South Africa, yet we didn't see any of that where we lived. And we wanted to.

It often feels easier to recognize and rely on God in a third-world country. Maybe it is because the needs in Africa are so great. People are poor, sick, and dying. They have physical needs that must be met, and quickly, just so they can survive. Perhaps they are more willing to turn to God for help because they lack resources. In the Western world, we are wealthier and have infrastructure, resources, and programs available to help us. Maybe the abundance of these things keeps us from feeling like we really need God. We believe in Jesus, know a little about Him, and ask Him to bless us, but I feel like it's hard to find many people who are wholeheartedly living their lives to serve Him and care for others, like He tells us to.

What if, in fact, we are the ones who are poor?

What would happen if we humbled ourselves, surrendered, and became desperate for God's help? Would we see Him working through signs and wonders? Would our faith be stronger and our God more active?

# Thirty

## COME, HOLY SPIRIT

...

In February 2016, I attended a meeting where an anointed teacher taught about the baptism of the Holy Spirit. This member of the Trinity was still a mystery to me, something I was confused about and sort of intimidated by. I hadn't heard a lot about being baptized in or filled with the Holy Spirit, yet this man's testimony was undeniably amazing. At the end of the meeting, the leader walked around the room, touched each of us, and prayed for us. As he did so, the atmosphere in the room changed. It began to feel slow, heavy, and thick.

When he placed his hands on me to pray, something happened. I began to feel things in my physical body, things I had read or heard about but had never experienced myself. My face felt intensely hot, my palms were wet, and I was slowly rocking back and forth. He spoke prophetically over me, and though I had heard other believers speak similar things, this man didn't know me at all. His words confirmed the visions and promises God had placed in my heart about where He was leading me.

I couldn't believe God had gone to such lengths to speak to me, through this man I had never met. I felt seen and known and validated by my heavenly Father, and the whole experience was so intimate. My faith in God skyrocketed, and I left there encouraged and with an even stronger desire for Him. I began poring over Scripture, reading all the books about the Holy Spirit that I could get my hands on, and praying with Spirit-filled believers on a regular basis. I discovered it was so important to be with other people who understood what I was learning and experiencing.

Two days after that meeting, I was still on a spiritual high. Up early in the morning, I sat in my green chair and sipped my coffee, enjoying my quiet time with God. As I studied about baptism and the filling of the Holy Spirit, I felt the Lord tell me to write this down in my journal:

*There is more. The people around you need to know that there is more. They've stopped short. Tell them there is more. They are deceived. Enemy wants to keep them where they are. They're stuck. Free them. I will use you. Your time will come. Keep pressing in. Huge crowds. You will tell them.*

I didn't know exactly what that meant or what it was going to look like; I didn't have a clear picture of where we were headed or what He was going to ask of me. I just knew that I believed Him and wanted to align my whole life to that belief. As Randy Clark says:

*God begins by preparing our hearts, turning us away from the things of this world and creating in us a great and desperate desire for Himself. He answers the cry of our hearts by drawing us deeper into relationship with Him, and then He touches us so profoundly that we are forever uprooted from our old lives and replanted by streams of living water, where we bear fruit in season. He causes us to prosper and produce fruit for His Kingdom.*[5]

## • WHAT IF? •

In the United States, we hardly ever hear people talking about the last miracle they witnessed, or any miracle they witnessed. Why is that when Mark 16:15–18 is the mission Jesus set for the church?

*Go into all the world and preach the Good News to everyone. Anyone who believes and is baptized will be saved. But anyone who refuses to believe will be condemned. These miraculous signs will accompany those who believe: They will cast out demons in my name, and they will speak in new languages. They will be able to handle snakes with safety, and if they drink anything poisonous, it won't hurt them. They will be able to place their hands on the sick, and they will be healed.*

There's a massive disconnect between the mandate set for the church two thousand years ago and what most of us experience on a daily basis. As we begin to recognize the differences, we find ourselves with questions: Was Jesus' mission reserved just for the early church in the book of Acts? Or was this mission given to *every* believer, every follower of Christ, even now? Should our everyday walk with God include casting out demons and healing the sick? Are we somehow missing the "more" of God—and is there more of God?

If Mark 16:15–18 is our mission, why aren't we casting out demons and healing the sick every day in the United States? It seems like healings and miracles are more prevalent in other countries,

---

5 Randy Clark, *There Is More! The Secret to Experiencing God's Power to Change Your Life* (Ada, MI: Chosen Books, 2013).

where people live in poverty. They don't have clean water and are dying from preventable diseases because they can't afford medical care. In a state of desperation, they have no option other than Jesus. They are aware of their need.

When we've "got it all together" and believe we have no needs, we run the risk of inching God out. We make Him a convenient addition to our lives, inviting Him into certain areas so He can bless what we're doing. But when we know our need for Him, when we have a healthy fear of Him and an understanding of who He really is and what He can do, He becomes everything to us.

God began to put on my heart a burden for the "poor in spirit," those who don't even realize they are in need. I read about the lukewarm church in Revelation 3:14–19 and felt a compassion and calling for them.

How would our lives change if we chose to believe God—really, truly believe Him? What if we believed everything Scripture says, taking it as ultimate truth above all else?

What if we truly committed our lives to Jesus Christ, surrendered our plans to Him, and followed Him? What would that look like? Wouldn't our priorities and desires be transformed? Wouldn't our everyday lives look different than they used to? Wouldn't they start to look less and less like the lives of unbelievers?

Wouldn't it be obvious that we were His disciples because of the way we lived, conducted ourselves, used our time, spent our money, and treated the people around us?

What would the church, the body of Christ, look like if every one of its members personally knew and had an intimate relationship with the living God?

# Thirty-One

## DEALING WITH THE FEAR OF MAN

...

I was head over heels in a *wonderful,* intimate relationship with God, and it was changing everything for me. Wanting to invite others along on this faith journey, I continued blogging, making videos, posting thoughts and quotes on social media, and pursuing opportunities to speak and share my testimony. I was in awe of all God was doing in my life and wanted to give Him glory and point others toward Him.

However, not everyone shared my excitement about my radical transformation. It came to my attention one day that some of my friends who followed me on social media thought I was getting carried away with my faith and were making fun of how outspoken I was. When I learned of this, I ran to Mark in his office, buried my face in his chest, and cried. If my "friends" were saying this stuff about me, I could only imagine how many others felt the same way. What if everyone was talking about me and making fun of me? I began to wonder if maybe I had gone too far and was revealing too much. Maybe

I should keep my faith more private. I *thought* I was being obedient by sharing what I was learning—but maybe I had misheard God.

"Mark," I whispered. "Do you think I should stop being so zealous? Maybe it would be better if I weren't so bold and public. I'm so sorry for any backlash you've been getting because your wife has been out there publicly proclaiming Jesus Christ."

"I love you and support you," he replied and held me in his arms until I was able to collect myself.

But my ego was bruised, and I wondered if I should slow down and be a little more cautious about what I shared. I messaged Gerda to seek her advice.

She replied, "Don't feel that, Kim. This walk is not about feeling but knowing. I have a word for you . . . Bind the enemy in Jesus' name and replace every thought with His Word. Jesus was persecuted. First sign you are called is the persecution. So you are on track, sister. Are you prepared to be ridiculed? Misunderstood? There is a price."

I was fine with being misunderstood, but if that was going to happen, I wanted to be sure I'd heard God correctly. Maybe this wasn't exactly what He was leading me to do. Was I too open with the world? Too honest maybe? "Should I slow down and be more cautious?" I asked.

If I did that, she answered, I would be joining the ranks of the lukewarm. "Do you want to be used? See this as a chance to die . . . to everything that will make you feel hurt, ashamed . . . dead to praise of man, dead to their criticism."

Toward the end of our conversation, she said, "Kim, you are called. Welcome to the next most amazing phase. No weapon formed against you will prosper. I am proud of you and Mark. You have a pure heart and God is using you, and it will be a mighty move of God. Don't back off. Don't shrink back."

Even when the people closest to me didn't understand what I was doing or didn't support me, I decided to be committed ultimately to

God. I knew He was calling me to be public with my faith, share with others, and be bold, with no concern for what people thought about me. Some people out there were being encouraged and inspired by my honesty, vulnerability, and authenticity, so I wasn't going to withdraw, censor myself, or fear what other people thought about me.

"The fear of man brings a snare, but he who trusts in the LORD will be exalted" (Prov. 29:25 NASB). The fear of man is a biblical category of fear that deals with the preoccupation of what people think of us. It can mean that we crave people's approval or we fear they will reject us. In other words, it puts people in the place of God in our lives and is a form of idolatry because ultimately, we should "worry" only about what the Lord thinks of us.

A snare is bait or a lure that leads to a trap, like something set out to capture small animals or birds. Some people live their entire lives boxed in. It's like they are trapped in a cage. They stay within society's set boundaries and feel safe and secure there; they are afraid to reach out, to stretch and leave their comfort zones. But their fear restrains and defeats them. Though they may feel safe, they are imprisoned and shackled; they are actually afraid of freedom. Others are focused on impressing people and seeking their approval. Maybe they need to be the center of attention or the life of the party. They constantly desire recognition, admiration, and praise. So wrapped up in others' opinions of them, they fear rejection and failure and are masking deep insecurity.

The only way to overcome the fear of man is to decide to fear the Lord and nothing else. We shouldn't be *afraid* of God, but we should possess a healthy reverence for Him. It should matter most what *He* thinks of us. This becomes easier when we're in proper relationship with Him, realizing how big and powerful He is. If we've made the opinions of other people in our lives too big, we've made God too small.

One day we will all stand before the judgment seat of Christ. In His presence, we will crumble at His glory and power. His goodness and love will overwhelm us. His beautiful, piercing eyes will expose everything we've ever done or left undone, everything we've said or left unsaid. In that moment, it won't matter at all what people thought of us. All that will matter is that Christ truly knows us, loves us, and died for us. If we're going to be concerned about something, we should spend our lives focused on pleasing the Lord, walking in obedience, and glorifying His name.

Coincidentally, while I was working through all of this in my personal life, I happened to be studying John 21:15–19 (NIV):

*When they had finished eating, Jesus said to Simon Peter, "Simon son of John, do you love me more than these?"*

*"Yes, Lord," he said, "you know that I love you."*

*Jesus said, "Feed my lambs."*

*Again Jesus said, "Simon son of John, do you love me?"*

*He answered, "Yes, Lord, you know that I love you."*

*Jesus said, "Take care of my sheep."*

*The third time he said to him, "Simon son of John, do you love me?"*

*Peter was hurt because Jesus asked him the third time, "Do you love me?" He said, "Lord, you know all things; you know that I love you."*

*Jesus said, "Feed my sheep. Very truly I tell you, when you were younger you dressed yourself and went where you wanted; but when you are old you will stretch out your hands, and someone else will dress you and lead you where you do not want to go." Jesus said this to indicate the kind of death by which Peter would glorify God. Then he said to him, "Follow me!"*

Like me, Peter was beginning to discover deep inside just how much he really did love the Lord. But he didn't realize it until Jesus persisted with His probing questions.

When the Lord asks us questions, they always reveal the truth to us about ourselves, and He never asks questions until the perfect time. God used Gerda, at just the right time in my walk with Him, to back me into the corner and ask me those piercing questions about my love for Him. It helped me to realize just how deep my love for Him was.

# Thirty-Two

## A TOUCH OF GOD

• • •

A couple of days later, I went to a conference at a local church because the conference's purpose intrigued me: to provide powerful teaching and offer a life-changing encounter with the Holy Spirit.

During worship, we were singing a song about revival and wanting it to come in a completely new way. In that moment, I felt God begin speaking to me.

"Revival is already here," He said and explained that it would come in greater power when we are on our knees. It requires humility and great faith, and we can't be bound by the fear of man. He told me to have laser focus on Him and not to be distracted by the things of this world. I needed to look to Him instead of looking left or right.

The next night Heidi Baker was speaking, and though I was excited to see and hear her again, I wasn't expecting to experience too much after the last time, when I had gone to see her in Oklahoma. In other words, I was trying not to get my hopes up. I sat all the way in the back, in the corner of the sanctuary.

During worship that night, I asked God to speak to me and confirm if He wanted to use my life to bring revival. Heidi got up on stage, and I wrote down the first words she said after her prayer: "There's been prophecy of worldwide revival. Who will prepare in prayer, worship, making a place where people could come home? Position yourself in wholehearted abandonment to the Holy Spirit."

I couldn't control my hand; it became impossible to stay inside the lines on the page. My writing was getting bigger and messier with every letter I wrote, and I began to realize I felt like I was drunk. About two minutes after Heidi walked out on stage, a force came over me. That was truly what it felt like. I suddenly stood up and dropped my journal on the floor. Walking around the seats, I headed right down the center aisle toward Heidi as she spoke to the crowd. I kept thinking to myself, *What am I doing? Everyone is looking at me! What am I going to do when I get up to the stage? I don't know, but I can't stop!*

When I got up to the front, I lay down flat on my face on the ground, right there in front of the sanctuary, in front of Heidi and everyone else. She didn't even skip a beat. She just kept talking. Honestly, I think she's probably used to things like this happening around her.

I stayed there on the floor, face down to the ground, arms spread out over my head, the entire time she spoke. It was at least an hour. I couldn't move. It felt like there was a heavy, weighted blanket on top of me. I could hear everything she was saying and even laughed at her jokes, but I could not get up.

At the end of the service, she prayed for the Holy Spirit to come and for His "fire to fall" on the place where we were. At one point, someone on her prayer team came and laid their hand on my back, and it felt like burning coals. As soon as they took their hand off me, the heat went away. I continued to lie there until after Heidi was done speaking and the conference was over. Eventually I was able to start moving but slowly. Everything was a blur around me, and the world seemed to be moving at a snail's pace. I looked around and was astonished to see dozens of people lying all around me, all over the floor in the front of the church.

When I could, I stumbled to my car in a fog and sat there in stillness for a few minutes before driving home. I climbed right into bed and fell asleep in that state of peace, filled with calm and quiet.

Early the next morning, I began to do some light research on the meaning of revival. I learned it basically means an improvement in the condition or strength of something, or what happens when something becomes popular, active, or important again. In other words, it's a spiritual *reawakening.* Revival invigorates and deepens faith; it opens a person's eyes to the truth in a new way. It's a fresh start, a clean slate, a new beginning. Revival happens when the Holy Spirit draws back the veil the world has cast over the truth and restores fellowship with God. The evidence of revival is a great outpouring of the Holy Spirit upon believers.

Revival isn't necessarily some "special happening" that takes place at an event or location. Revival is happening *now,* in the hearts of His people, in quiet moments with the Lord. People are being transformed and ignited to go out into their families, neighborhoods, communities, cities, and counties. We can't just wait, anticipating that someone else to bring revival—it comes from the Holy Spirit within each of us.

Jesus said, "The kingdom of heaven is at hand" (Matt. 4:17 NASB). The Kingdom is wherever the power and glory of God are manifested, witnessed to, and confessed. The Kingdom has arrived; it is here in our midst and it is now.

# Thirty-Three

## INTERCESSION

...

In April 2016, I boarded a plane, alone, for my eleventh trip to South Africa. If you'd told me ten years ago that I would be heavily involved with a nonprofit in *Africa*, of all places, and that I would be traveling back and forth regularly, even leading groups of women there and adopting a son from there—I would have thought you'd lost your mind.

But there I was, traveling all by myself to work with Acres of Love, staying in hotels by myself, using Uber to get around, hosting major donors, visiting the kids, holding meetings, and speaking at a dedication. I loved it.

My favorite part of overseas trips is when there's "margin" in my itinerary. I do a meticulous job planning my time: flights, hotels, transport, meetings, and dinners. But I love, love, love the parts of the day when there is free time, and I can allow the Holy Spirit to lead me. I get to be open and available to new adventures, new relationships, new things God wants to show me and teach me. Often I discover that the waiters I meet, the drivers I get to know, the experiences that were not on the itinerary—all these things can leave the biggest mark on me. I may not have scheduled them into my trip, but God did. He knows the people I need to meet, the things my eyes need to see, the parts of my heart that need breaking, and the lasting lessons He wants me to take home when I leave. He knows what will transform me, deepen my faith, and bless others.

On this particular trip, I had quite a bit of margin—one full day—and was excited to see what God had in store for me. A few weeks earlier, I'd read an article Gerda had sent me about a hospital in South Africa. The article highlighted a surgeon who expressed how overwhelming and depressing the job can be. Most of the children he works with live in utter poverty and are burned in shack fires. The parents frequently don't come back to visit, and the children are simply abandoned there in the hospital. This wasn't something that shocked me all that much because I'd been working with orphans in South Africa long enough to know the situation is bleak. But something about this article really impacted me. I sensed that God was telling me to go there, to that city, to that specific hospital, to that specific burn unit, and just be among the staff, the patients, and parents. I felt Him leading me to sit with them, hold babies, comfort them, pray for them, and encourage them.

I replied something like this: "Of course. I would *love* to do that. But I can't just jump on a plane and go. It's expensive! If Gerda invites me to go to South Africa to do some work for Acres of Love, and she pays for the trip, then I will go to that hospital."

I wrote about this interaction in my journal as proof, just in case it happened that Gerda did end up inviting me.

Well, about eight hours later, I got a text from her: "Kim, won't you please join me in SA in April?" She added later in the conversation, "And of course we will pay for it." So I emailed the hospital, told them the story, and made a plan to spend an entire day there on my upcoming trip.

Talk about margin—an entire day to be spent at this hospital. My goal was to follow the Lord's leading in every area possible: who I should spend time with, who I should pray for, who I should read the Bible to, who I should lead to the Lord, who I should hold, who I should hug or cry with or laugh with. My prayers leading up to that day, April 6, focused on my ability to be a willing and available vessel for the Lord to use as He pleased. I didn't want to go in with any agenda concerning what should happen. Instead, I wanted to be sensitive to the Spirit.

To prepare for my time, I began searching God's Word for appropriate Scriptures I might share, applicable stories I might read, some powerful words I might include in prayer, etc.

I have learned that God just loves these rare opportunities to work in and through us. When we are most uncomfortable, vulnerable, incapable, ill equipped, and unprepared—that's when He can really do His thing. In those situations we are most willing to admit we don't have all the answers, that we don't know what to do or what to say. We finally give up the control we thought we had and ask God for help. We invite Him in, beg for His guidance and wisdom, allow Him to move and work and show off. I found that even the simple act of preparing myself for this day was a blessing. I was about to go spend time in a burn unit that was filled with sadness, impossible situations, and heartache—I needed God. That's a humbling place to be, to need God so desperately, and it's right where He wants us, looking to Him for everything we need.

I thought I was getting involved with this hospital to be a blessing to them, but even before I got there, I realized I was the one being blessed. The understanding of how desperate I was for God to work in and through me filled my heart with hope. As the apostle Paul wrote, "That's why I take pleasure in my weakness, and in the insults, hardships, persecutions, and troubles that I suffer for Christ. For when I am weak, then I am strong" (2 Cor. 12:10). It is *good* for our hearts when we respond to invitations from that "still, small voice," extend ourselves, get out of our comfort zones, and serve others. This may be especially true when we feel we aren't equipped to do it. Apart from Him we can do nothing, just like Jesus said (John 15:5).

When I arrived at the hospital, my heart moved as I came upon a little boy who was crying. He must have been about seven years old. I couldn't tell exactly why he was at the hospital or how long he had been lying in that bed. It seemed he wasn't even producing tears anymore; his cry was sort of empty, like a long, unenergetic wail that had become a habit. I could feel the desperation in it, the hopelessness. It was like he didn't really believe anyone was going to respond.

I saw a lot of that while I was there. I walked every hall in every ward of that hospital and looked at every single patient. I saw tiny babies in incubators, children so burned that they were completely covered in gauze bandages and all you could see was their dark little eyes peering through; I saw several kids with swollen heads, bellies distended, limbs crippled, infections oozing.

Frustration built within me. My whole intention for visiting that hospital was to touch people, lay hands on them, pray for them, talk to them, encourage them, and bring them some comfort, hope, and strength. But I was under strict instruction from the staff not to do anything like that. I was not supposed to deeply engage anyone, nor could I ask questions or linger. All I could do was offer up quiet, nearly silent prayers as I walked past beds. Whispering, "Jesus, Jesus," I trusted that He knew what was happening to my heart, that He heard the thoughts racing through my mind, that He received my pleas for His presence, healing, peace, and comfort.

On the long drive back to my hotel, I wrestled with a strong sense of uselessness. It seemed like such a waste of a day. I had come all this way for that? God told me to go there . . . but for what? I didn't get to *do* anything. I didn't help, didn't make a bit of difference. Here I had intentionally gotten up early that morning (despite my jet lag!), prepared coffee in my room, and prayed, read, and studied in preparation.

Intercessory prayer means to fill up what is lacking. It's putting yourself in God's place and having His mind and perspective. Our work can have such close contact with the Lord that we have His mind about everything. Instead of trying to patch things up, we get to pray the person into contact with the very life of God. I was armed and ready to walk through the hospital doors that day and be the hands and feet of Jesus. But I didn't get to touch a single child, didn't get to console one mother, didn't bring hope or encouragement or comfort to anyone.

Oswald Chambers says we should "be aware of bringing our personal sympathies into the presence of God and demanding that He does what we ask."[6] As I sipped my coffee in my hotel bed that morning, I didn't see how those words applied to me at all, but that night on the same hotel bed, I saw how they applied specifically to me! I was so disappointed because I'd wanted to be able to do something tangible, something that could be humanly measured, that made an impact in the moment. I wanted to see the results of my effort and feel good about making a difference to those poor children in the hospital.

But I realized God had me brought to the hospital and put me among those people so I could simply walk through the halls past the children and cry out in a desperate whisper, "Jesus. Jesus." He used me to usher in His presence into that horrific place and to trust Him for the rest.

---

6 Chambers, *My Utmost for His Highest.*

# · WHAT IF? ·

God is the only One who can truly make a difference. If we really understood and believed this at a deep level, what would happen? What would our lives look like if we believed that our prayers of intercession made an eternal impact on the people He brought before us? I think we wouldn't feel disappointed and defeated when our sympathetic actions didn't seem to make a bit of difference. Instead, we would trust that bringing these people before God's throne offered healing, peace that surpasses all understanding, and salvation for eternal life.

If we knew the power of our prayers, I don't think we would ever show up in a seemingly hopeless situation and fail to realize we were sent there for a divine purpose.

# Thirty-four

## SPIRITUAL BATTLE

...

I hardly ever sleep in, even when I'm in Africa. During this trip, I'd been setting my alarm early so I could get up, make a little coffee in my hotel room, pray, read the Bible, and prepare for the day. But one night as I was setting my alarm, I felt that I should sleep in and do my typical quiet time over breakfast. So I set my alarm for a later time than I usually would.

I woke up naturally early that morning and contemplated getting up. But I managed to pray myself back to sleep and had a vivid dream about Gerda and Anna, one of our house moms. About an hour later when my alarm went off, I climbed out of bed and got in the shower. I couldn't stop thinking about the dream, so I sent a message to Anna, told her I had dreamed about her being sick, and asked if she was okay. Here is our conversation:

*Me: How are you this morning? I had a dream that you were sick and overwhelmed. Just want to make sure that you feel well rested and healthy.*

*Anna: Please pray for me. Still in my room, haven't been to the kitchen. Yes, you are right, my sister.*

*Me: Praying, in Jesus' name, that you are healed completely right away. Trusting God who called you to this work on this very day to fill you with the strength and energy that you need to accomplish His will. In Jesus' name, bind the enemy who is trying to keep you down. Nothing formed against you will prosper.*

*Anna: Tears running down my cheeks. Thank you for praying for me. I thank the power of the Holy Spirit that connects us.*

*Me: In my dream, you were wearing bright, beautiful floral pajamas and we came to visit you as you were trying to put everyone to bed. You fainted into Gerda's arms and had a fever. She was kissing your cheeks over and over.*

The dream impacted my friend Anna, and she told me, "God is with me. He knows everything about me. I am so amazed by the dream and it is true."

I was in awe of how God would use my dream as a starting point for giving my friend what she needed. He is so faithful and knows every detail of our lives. "I love you so much," I wrote. "You will get better right away."

"Because God showed you, sister, I believe I have conquered in Jesus' name!" Anna replied.

Five hours later, I texted her again to see how she was feeling.

"I praise God for His instant healing," she answered. "He touched me and something happened." My friend was completely healed—and my dream got to be a part of it.

This was a victory for sure. But not everything that happened on this trip felt victorious to me.

A few days later, I had just finished a quick meeting in the lobby bar with a few other Acres of Love team members. We'd been comparing notes and confirming plans to host the many donor partners from the United States who were en route to Cape Town to dedicate our Special Needs Advancement Center.

When I got back to my room, I realized it was late morning at home, so I called my family through video chat. Mark was sitting in the car alone, trying to take a little break from the kids while they were camping at the beach. His body language said it all; he was frustrated and disappointed with their behavior, and I could sense the heaviness of his spirit. I wished I could have been there to help, to share the burden and relieve him. But there was nothing I could do from my hotel room in South Africa. All I could offer were words of apology and encouragement. When we got off the phone, he had to head back into the trenches where he would be stuck for another seven days while I was alone on the other side of the world.

And there the battle began. I broke down in tears and the guilt nearly overcame me. Was it wrong for me to be in South Africa for this length of time, so far away from the kids? Was I wrong to be this involved with Acres of Love, this devoted to my work with the organization? Maybe I was being selfish and neglecting my family, opting out of my responsibilities as a wife and mom. Perhaps God hadn't really called me to this work after all, and I needed to reevaluate and refocus. If it was true I had completely screwed up, then I should shorten my trip and go home early.

The questions pounded me, and as I wept, my heart began to hurt with such intensity that it felt like I was literally being crushed. I became aware of how very alone I was in that room, so far away from home and very much in a foreign country all by myself. I pulled the covers up over my head, sobbed into the pillow, and begged God to help me. Eventually I cried myself to sleep.

When I woke up in the morning, I made myself a cup of coffee and spent some quiet time with the Lord. It's always easier to see clearly in daylight. Looking back over what had happened the night before, I began to realize I'd been in a spiritual battle. The enemy had tried to tell me I was selfish, a terrible wife, a neglectful mother, that I misheard God and shouldn't be away from my family.

But none of that was true. I *knew* God had sent me to South Africa.

Slowly I began to sense that I was in South Africa alone—without Sue, Gretchen, or Mark—for a reason. I realized God was preparing me for something. He had allowed the enemy to put me in a vulnerable position, which forced me to pray, seek, and desperately look to God for answers and strength. In addition to serving Acres of Love and furthering my commitment to Gerda, the kids, and the staff, I was there to learn and prepare for the future assignment God had for me. I was there to hear from Him.

After that morning, I felt the Lord's tangible presence the rest of my time in South Africa. Everywhere I went, I could feel Him with me. It seemed like I connected with every person I spoke to on a supernatural level. God spoke to me clearly on countless occasions and proved Himself real, faithful, and accessible. I felt renewed, confident, and like I had been given a certain authority. Things were different.

As my time in South Africa drew to an end, I prayed that upon my return home to my busy life as a wife and mom, I wouldn't lose the awareness of the constant presence of the Holy Spirit. I could only imagine what life would be like in Orange County if I moved through my days with this same knowing that God was in me, with me, and wanted to use me.

# · WHAT IF? ·

These amazing encounters aren't reserved just for Africa. God is in Southern California as much as He is in distant countries. His heart is for the people at home too.

What would happen if I lived my life at home the way I lived it in South Africa: yielding to the Holy Spirit, walking in my authority in Christ, being a willing and available vessel to everyone I came in contact with?

Perhaps if I carried that same boldness and sense of calling, more people around me would encounter God. Maybe I would see astonishing moves of God if I treated my own city like a mission field instead of reserving myself for the foreign places I traveled to. What if living this way enabled me to make a greater impact?

# Thirty-five

## NICE TRY, SATAN

...

A few days after my return from South Africa, I heard my five-year-old daughter, Avery, walk into my room. Like she often did, she climbed into bed next to me, snuggled in close, and we went back to sleep.

A couple of hours later, I woke up to a warm, wet feeling on my back and realized Avery had peed in the bed. I rolled over to look at her and paused. Her eyes were wide open, locked into a fierce position staring at the ceiling; her entire body was rigid. She was having a seizure.

I screamed to wake up Mark, who was sleeping on the other side of her. "Avery's having a seizure! Call 911!"

I jumped up on my knees and hovered over her, praying into her ear. Mark woke the other kids and called Gretchen to come stay with them.

Minutes later, we had firefighters and paramedics surrounding our bed. When they couldn't get her seizure to stop, they put me on a gurney with her in my arms, carried us down the stairs to the ambulance, and rushed us to the emergency room.

Avery had three very long seizures that morning, and we ended up in the ICU. I lay next to her in the hospital bed and snuggled up as close as I could get while she slept. As the minutes crept by, I took long, deep breaths of the smell of her skin, stroked her beautiful blonde hair, and studied her gorgeous little face.

Being in the hospital hadn't been on my calendar for that day. I'd planned on going to church with my family, having some lunch, making a trip to the grocery store to stock up on healthy food for the week, and having dinner at a friend's house. I didn't realize my day was going to start at 3:30 a.m. when my beautiful little daughter had her first of three horrifying seizures. I was not anticipating a 911 call and an ambulance ride, the emergency room, CAT scans, blood work, the ICU, EEGs, and a traumatizing spinal tap. It wasn't what I had planned whatsoever.

Life is usually what happens while we're busy making plans. None of us have any idea what's around the next corner. Only God knows what the future holds, and He is never surprised, never caught off guard. He's never late. He's never early. He's always right on time. Could I trust Him even in a hospital room? Even in times like this?

For hours, I prayed, read Scriptures to my daughter, played worship music, and sang in her ear. I spoke life into the situation and chose to trust God with all of it, even the things I didn't understand, because I knew He was good. His plans for Avery and our family were good. His ways were higher than our ways. The situation in that pediatric ICU room didn't offer all the answers, but I knew I didn't need them. The only answer I actually needed was that God loved me and loved my precious Avery even more than I did. So I gave her to Him and I trusted that He had her.

Two days later, I was still sitting in that hospital room with Avery. Reading my daily devotional, I came upon this sentence: "But if we will stay true to God, God will take us through an ordeal that will serve to bring us into a better knowledge of himself."[7] During this time, which was surely an ordeal, Mark repeatedly mentioned how rock solid my faith was. It was interesting to me as well, because I wasn't filled with fear or doubt. Instead of feeling weak or timid, I had full confidence that everything was going to be okay, that God was with us, that His plans for our family were good. I didn't consciously make a decision to feel or act this way; it happened naturally—a knowing deep within me. By this point, I'd spent so much time studying the Word and getting to know God personally. I was following Jesus, obeying Him, encountering Him, and getting to experience how faithful, merciful, and loving He is. I had changed. The Holy Spirit had transformed me somewhere along the way, and I found that I had unshakable faith.

When we start taking this faith stuff seriously, when we really start believing it and living it out, we become a threat to Satan and his plan to steal, kill, and destroy (John 10:10) the abundant life God has planned for us. Taking up with Jesus is an invitation for the enemy to attack. We are in a spiritual battle, and aligning with Jesus puts us in opposition to Satan. Even though we can't physically see our attacker, he is relentless in his efforts to take us down. This is good to remember, so we aren't caught by surprise.

At the same time, we have nothing to fear because in Christ we have all authority over the enemy. "If God is for us, who can be against us?" Romans 8:31 asks, and the apostle Paul adds in verse 37, "We are more than conquerors" (NIV).

When Avery was on the mend and back home again, I began to feel a need to announce to the spirit world where my home and family stood. I wanted to make it clear, so the enemy understood perfectly

---

7 Chambers, *My Utmost for His Highest.*

that we loved and served the Lord; we were committing our whole lives to God and were declaring our allegiance in the ongoing spiritual battle.

One early, dark morning while the kids were still asleep, Mark and I anointed our home. We sat together in the family room and prayed, "Father, in the name of Jesus Christ, we ask that You would sanctify everything within the perimeters of our property and that everything would be made holy. We dedicate this property to You and ask that You, Holy Spirit, would continually flow over and perpetually bless this property."

We went through every room together, marking the doorways with oil and dedicating our home, marriage, and children to God.

# Thirty-Six

## GOD SPEAKS

...

For many years, Gretchen had been friends with a woman named Irene who used to be their family's nanny. Full of faith, Irene was a gifted prayer warrior and intercessor. One day in August, Gretchen suggested we go over to Irene's to learn from her and pray with her.

So Sue, Gretchen, and I went to her apartment and had an amazing time with her and her two friends, Martina and Kianny. Irene and Martina spoke mostly Spanish, so Kianny translated for us. We listened to their stories, were encouraged by their faith, and prayed with them for hours.

At one point in the evening, the three of them gathered around me in the living room and started praying for me in Spanish. They grew louder and more engaged in the prayer until they were yelling, jumping up and down, putting their hands on me, and shaking. They spoke rapidly in Spanish, sharing with me what they were hearing from the Lord—prophetic words of exhortation that Kianny translated.

"It's not a calling," they told me. "It's a ministry. You will have grace in the Word, and people will listen to you. You will go places, travel, and your feet will walk places you never imagined. Doors will open for you. Even the doors that everyone says won't, they will. You have a prophetic gift. You need to be in a church that moves in gifts of the Spirit. They will develop quickly. You have words in the womb. You have power in prayer. You hear God. It's going to be okay. You have an angel with you. It's His testimony. Your words are like arrows shooting out of your mouth."

The energy in the room was so thick and powerful that it was nearly overwhelming. At one point as Irene prayed for me, she began shaking uncontrollably, and I fell over backward and just lay on the floor weeping. I felt like this was the beginning of something new, that everything was going to be different from that point on. Something shifted inside of me as I wept in surrender and received what they were saying to me.

As they spoke these prophetic words over me, I kept saying, "I know. I know." As radical as their words were, somehow they were no surprise. It was like the Lord had already told me these things, and as a result, I had a deep sense of what He was calling me to. I realized I had been hearing God correctly all along; He used these women who didn't know me to reassure me. I felt so loved that He would go to these lengths to speak to me and reveal Himself to me through these women of faith.

The Lord is real and alive, and He pursues us. He loves us so much and is eager to communicate with us in various ways just how precious we are to Him. He has plans for us and wants to use us; He wants to reach others through us and bring glory to Himself.

Later that week, my mom had a bad fall and broke her back. Early in the morning before I went to visit her at the hospital, I was praying for her and remembered how Martina had told me I had the gift of prophecy. So I asked God for a word for my mom—a special message

I could deliver to her from Him. I wrote down what I felt He was telling me and ended up with several pages of things to say to her. Specifically, I felt like He told me she would receive eternal life that day.

But this was hard for me. My parents weren't Christians, and I wasn't exactly sure how they would respond to "a word from the Lord" for them. I knew God was telling me to read to my mom what I had written down. I was nervous, but He told me it wasn't about my feelings; He was sending me on assignment and I had a job to do. It was like a business transaction, and my mom would accept it.

In her hospital room, I told my parents that I wanted to share something with them that God had told me. I read the message to them, and as soon as I had said the last word, without emotion or hesitation, I asked if they wanted to respond to the Lord's invitation of salvation.

Quietly and calmly, they both said, "Yes."

I prayed with them. We spent more time visiting, and I spoke with her doctor. When I left the room to head home, I was surprised that I wasn't more emotional or excited. I'd been dreaming about leading them to the Lord for years, and it had finally happened. Why didn't I feel anything?

Slowly I began to understand it was because I had known what would happen. God had clearly told me that morning what He was about to do.

Once again, I was blown away by His faithfulness and love. He had been so generous with me, speaking to me about my mom and assuring me that she was ready. I took a risk and followed what I felt God had given me to share with my mom, and as a result, both my parents began a relationship with Him.

# · WHAT IF? ·

What if I really believed what I felt God was telling me about who I was in Christ and how He wanted to use my life? What if I acted like I believed it?

Once God told me about the gifts He'd given me and the calling on my life, what was I supposed to do? How does a person respond when the Lord says, "Hey, this is you"? If I wanted to walk according to my calling, what did that look like?

I knew I needed to start acting in a way that aligned with the prophetic words I'd been given. This meant pursuing opportunities to travel, writing and speaking boldly, praying for people, and trusting what I felt I was hearing from God. I needed to believe that He really wanted to use my life and, consequently, be willing and available to serve Him.

# Thirty-Seven

## OIL AND GOLD

• • •

In September 2016, my friend Sue and I took a trip up to Redding, California. For about six months, I had been trying to find really good teaching on the Holy Spirit and His gifts because I wanted to understand more of what I was personally experiencing with God. Bethel is well known for being a community of believers who are truly moving in the Spirit and experiencing regular healings, miracles, signs, and wonders. I was going there specifically to attend a writing workshop, and Sue went with me as my traveling companion.

On the plane, she and I discussed how badly we wanted to encounter more of God. We wanted to see the healings happen right in front of us, experience God manifesting Himself to people, and be powerfully moved by the Holy Spirit.

"I better see something this weekend," I told Sue. "I'm so tired of asking to see more and then nothing good happens when I'm there!"

After we'd arrived in Redding and checked into our hotel, I received an unexpected email—my writing workshop had been cancelled due to low registration. *What?* As frustrating as it was, I felt a flicker of excitement because both Sue and I realized that God had brought us up here for another reason, something we would soon discover.

The workshop instructor, Jen, ended up offering to meet with me privately since I'd made the trip. We scheduled a breakfast meeting for two days later. With our newfound time, Sue and I decided to go check out the Bethel Healing Rooms. She had some GI issues, and I struggled with an autoimmune disease, so we drove to the church early the next morning, filled out the paperwork, and waited with about thirty other people to go into the main room.

As we waited, an older man gave a brief teaching on healing.

"Receive healing," he said. "Receive the Father's love. This is your time to encounter the Father. You are counted worthy to be loved and worthy to be healed."

He stretched out his arms in front of him and opened up his hands, showing us his palms that glistened in the light. He said that oil often appeared on his hands when he prayed for people for healing.

I leaned over and whispered to Sue, "I want that!"

He told us to put our hands in a posture of receiving, and then he began to pray for us. "My hands are very hot. You might begin to feel heat in your hands."

*I don't feel any heat,* I thought. *I wish I did. I do feel a strong tingling sensation in my right hand. That's weird.*

"Maybe you feel a tingling sensation," the man said.

I opened my eyes in surprise and looked at him. Then I looked down to check out my right hand. A light layer of oil covered my palm. I pulled my hand close to my face and studied it. It looked like oil was oozing out of the cracks and crevices and pooling up on my palm and fingers. Then I noticed that my hand looked all shimmery, like there was a layer of gold glitter dust on it. I stared at it, squinting my eyes and looking at it from all different angles. Lifting my head, I looked around the room, wondering if someone had somehow sprinkled this stuff on my hand and I hadn't felt it. I looked up at the ceiling—was something up there rigged to drop oil and gold dust? But there were no schemers in sight. I couldn't believe it!

Elbowing Sue, I showed her my right hand and asked if she could see what I was seeing.

"I can," she whispered.

"Are you sure?" I whispered back. "Can you really, really see it?"

In amazement herself, she assured me she could. I checked out the room again to see if anyone else was experiencing the same thing. Here I was freaking out, but everybody else was sitting there contained and quiet. I rubbed my hand on my journal to see if the oil would come off. It did. There was evidence of it right there on the page. I kept staring at my hand and trying to make sense of what was happening as the facilitators led our group into the main room.

A young girl approached me. She walked me over to two gentlemen who prayed for my thyroid and began to speak prophetically over me.

"It's time!" they said. They told me I was stepping into a healing ministry, and one of them said, "I see a cable going up from the top of your head. It's pulling you up, straightening you and putting everything into alignment."

Even as they were praying and talking to me, I felt like I was being lifted up. The sensation was so *real* that I found myself rising higher and higher on my tiptoes until it wasn't physically possible for me to push up any higher. I felt like I was levitating, like I was about to leave the ground. I even lost my balance because I was up so high on my toes.

After all of this, Sue and I went out for lunch and ordered much-needed glasses of wine. We went over everything that had just happened. What *was* all of that? What did it mean? And more important, what were we supposed to do now?

As we were talking, I started to get that tingling feeling in my right hand again. I looked down and found oil coming out of the creases of my hand and gold dust shimmering under the lights. I showed Sue and fumbled to grab my cell phone, so I could document this crazy phenomenon and show Mark.

Back at the hotel, I crawled under the covers and stayed there for a few hours. Later I called Mark and told him what was going on. I sent him the videos, and he was astonished and unsure, just like I was. I called Gerda, too, and shared the story with her. She laughed and celebrated that God had shown me His glory in this way.

When Sue and I went out for dinner that evening, we talked about how excited we were to go home and share with everyone how God had done the most unexpected, supernatural thing. We repeatedly said that we craved focus and a vision for what God was doing in our lives. In particular, I wanted these things for my book.

The next morning, we met the writing coach, Jen, for breakfast. She spent time with me brainstorming ideas for the book and providing me with the structure, vision, focus, and clarity I had just been telling Sue I needed to move forward with my writing and ministry.

As we were talking, I again felt that tingling sensation, and sure enough, my right hand was covered in oil and gold dust. Jen confirmed what I was seeing and experiencing, and she prayed for me, praising God for revealing Himself in this incredible way.

# Thirty-Eight

## REFINER'S FIRE

...

When I returned home from my time up at Bethel, I was so excited to share what had happened to me. My friends were clearly moved by the story of God manifesting Himself in this unique way. I received countless texts, calls, and emails from people saying they couldn't stop thinking about my hand; many of them weren't able to concentrate on anything else, and so they were looking for explanations in the Bible, doing research, reading articles, watching videos, and trying to figure out what it all meant. The sign and wonder that had happened to me was impacting others' faith. They were curious; some were encouraged and some were doubtful. But in the end, they were thinking about it, digging deeper and searching for answers. Isn't that what a "sign and wonder" is all about? It's like a sign in a warehouse that directs you where to go. God uses signs and wonders to draw our attention to Him and to direct and lead us.

Inside of me an undeniable fire blazed. I just wanted to sit at His feet, worship Him, pray, and study my Bible. I spent so much time on my knees, face to the ground as I wept, asking Him to show me more

189

of Himself. I felt desperate for Him to show up and reveal Himself to me again.

But a different type of fire was burning inside of me too. It was like all the things that competed with my intimacy with God—old desires, priorities, assumptions, mental and emotional blocks—were being reduced to ash. I wanted to get rid of anything that prevented me from having a power-filled, life-giving relationship with my heavenly Father. It was like I was being supernaturally refined. "For he will be like a blazing fire that refines metal . . . He will sit like a refiner of silver . . . so that they may once again offer acceptable sacrifices to the LORD" (Mal. 3:3). When metals are refined, the raw metal is heated in the fire until it melts. Impurities separate and rise to the surface so they can be skimmed off, leaving the pure metal behind. Without this process of heating and melting, purification can't occur.

As I thought about the ministry I was building, I didn't want to come up with some clever shtick to entertain, impress, or persuade an audience. I just wanted to share His words. I realized it wasn't my job to convince or transform anyone; I didn't need to run ahead and put together some big PR and marketing plan to promote myself and "gain a following" for God. He would open the right doors and bring the right people and the right message. He was responsible for the outcome. Tenderly and with love, He started to show me that parts of me were striving in my own strength instead of His. I was trying to push my own agenda, setting my own goals and standards of success, while He was the One doing the work, giving me the desire to serve Him in this way and the power to do anything worthwhile. All I had to do was walk in absolute surrender moment by moment. It was imperative that I stay connected to Him, the source, and be obedient.

As good as all of that sounds, the next season in my life proved to be a confusing time. On one hand, I had made a wholehearted commitment to God. I was learning so much so fast, was on an exciting adventure, and felt full of joy and purpose.

But on the other hand, I was frustrated that I wasn't making as much progress in other areas of my life. I had an intimate relationship with the Lord, and in my time with Him on the "mountaintop," everything was glorious. Then I would come down the mountain into my day-to-day life, and I would struggle as I navigated my relationships and responsibilities. A painful gap existed between how I thought my life should be and how it actually was. I struggled as a wife and mom and had a difficult time being the loving, patient, wise woman I knew God had called me to be. I wanted to be better and do better, but my flesh wasn't cooperating. How could I be filled with the Holy Spirit and not be more transformed and Christlike on a daily basis?

It certainly wasn't for lack of trying. I would get up every morning and ask God for His help, and then, armed with the best intentions, charge into my day with my family. But inevitably I would mess up and feel defeated, like I was letting everyone down. I really struggled to change my old ways. It was easy for me to love, serve, and pray for friends, strangers, and those who were suffering, but somehow it was hard to selflessly and sacrificially love the people in my own home. That was where I was the ugliest, where I felt the least like Christ. All I could do was ask God to take away this thing in me that felt like it needed to control, be right, and be in charge. I asked Him to reveal the dark places of my heart and show me my rebellion and pride. This, I quickly realized, was another way of choosing to surrender myself to Him.

And in that place of surrender, I found freedom. He began to slowly and tenderly teach me about true repentance, dying to self, forgiveness, and what it means to "resurrect" into brand-new life.

# Thirty-Nine

## WHAT NOT TO DO

...

In November 2016, after spending time in South Africa with Acres of Love, I flew to Mozambique with a few friends to visit Heidi Baker's ministry, Iris Global, in Pemba.

Thrilled to see another part of Africa, I was looking forward to blessing the people, being with Heidi, and seeing the work she was doing. I fully expected to see God move in miraculous ways.

While on the flight to Mozambique, I pondered the work I felt God was calling me to and wrote in my journal, *I will need God's compassion. I can't do anything in my own human flesh. God, give me Your eyes to see, Your heart to feel, Your wisdom to know, Your power to heal and save.*

Two days later, I was hot, dirty, hungry, and pretty darn miserable. I had thought I would love this. I had even pictured myself living in Africa someday among the poor as I loved and served them. But this was awful. I couldn't stand being in Mozambique. Guilt gnawed at me because I couldn't bring myself to enjoy, let alone embrace, the missionary lifestyle I was exposed to.

One day I sneaked away from the group for some quiet time with the Lord. As I sat in a thatched gazebo and prayed, I felt the Lord lovingly remind me that it's not all about me. It's about loving the people He puts in front of me. His love in me will flow through me, and He is looking for surrendered vessels through whom He can love His people.

"Would You baptize me with Your love?" I whispered to Him, wanting His love to compel me. I asked Him for the gift of compassion.

During this trip, we spent a few hours in an orphanage for babies. So many little children depended on the care of only two women. Several children were sitting down in wet diapers, and I was overcome with sadness. What would the future be like for these babies? Was living at the orphanage really helping them? They were considered the lucky ones because they were rescued; they were safe now and had food and a bed. But there was no love, no bonding, and no attachment with the few tired and overwhelmed staff sitting around on the cement floor.

One girl about seven years old was lying facedown in the middle of the room among all the babies.

"What about this one?" we asked.

They told us her name was Magdalena, and she wasn't doing well. It appeared she had cerebral palsy. Her hand was bleeding all over the place, and right in front of us, she began having a seizure. When we picked her up, we found that she had soiled her pants and had a fever. She was choking on the bandage that had been on her hand from the IV.

We sat with her on our laps as we tried to calm and soothe her. She shook and jerked uncontrollably, and foam spilled out of her mouth. Her eyes rolled back in her head. This went on for twenty minutes, and the staff didn't show any sense of urgency or concern.

Finally I took her cheeks in my hands, looked at her face, and said, "In the name of Jesus, I rebuke you, Satan. Get out of her right now, you spirit of epilepsy. I command this body to heal. I command this seizure to stop in Jesus' name."

She slowly began to calm, just a bit. Eventually she made eye contact with me, and her body stopped moving. She became still, quiet, calm, looking right back at me. After a couple of minutes, her body would stiffen again, and her eyes would lose focus and begin to roll. I would sternly say, "No! No! Be healed in Jesus' name." I took her in my lap, rocked her, and sang to her. The entire time we were there, she was peaceful and calm.

As we were about to leave, Magdalena again began to seize. My heart ached for her, and I didn't know what to do. A host of questions poured through me: What was going to happen to her? Where was God in this situation? Was this His plan for her life? How can there be so much suffering in the world, and what part did I play in helping to resolve it? How was I supposed to leave the orphanage and just walk away? Eventually I set that precious little child down and tearfully left her.

An hour later, I had taken a cold shower in a dirty bathroom and eaten another granola bar and more dried mango. Missionary life! But I was grateful to be clean with a full stomach.

My questions and sense of unrest didn't stop. Later in a worship service, I kept asking God to show me more of Himself, to speak to me, and to show up in a miraculous way that would rock my world. I asked for clarity, pleading with Him to tell me what He wanted to use me for. This trip was so difficult for me—why was I there? What did He want me to see, and what was I supposed to experience and learn?

In my spirit, I heard Him gently question me. "Why do you keep asking Me for yourself when there are so many in need?"

I met a pastor named Allan who was also from the United States. When I told him about the oil and gold dust God had given me, he took my hands in his, looked into my eyes, and said, "God gave you oil and gold dust three times, and you are asking for more? What are you waiting for? Start praying for people!"

Disappointed and a little ashamed that I wasn't enjoying my time in Mozambique more, I continued to struggle with the dirt, hunger, poverty, and need. For a while, I had thought God might call me to that kind of life, that it was a "greater calling" and somehow more romantic and dramatic to leave everything and follow God to Africa. So if I couldn't hack it as a missionary right now, how was I going to handle all the great things I thought God was calling me to? And if I *wasn't* called to Africa, what in the world was I supposed to do and where?

At one point, Heidi told us a story of when she was ministering to the people who lived in the dump. It was filthy, with flies all over the place, and the smell was foul. She said most people couldn't handle working there with her, but she actually loved the smell of the dump! It was because God had given her grace for that particular calling. She told us that our calling shouldn't be in a place we hate—but in a place we love. God created us uniquely and knows the desires of our hearts.

"What is your sweet spot?" Heidi asked. "That's where God is calling you."

*Oh,* I thought. God wasn't calling me to be a missionary in rural Africa. He wasn't expecting me to be just like Heidi or some other person, because He didn't create me to copy someone else. He created me with very specific gifts and talents, as well as the favor to use those things for Him, wherever and with whomever He chose.

My sweet spot, the time I feel most energized, alive, and useful, is when I am sharing with others what I have learned. I love to teach, encourage, empower, and disciple. God has already given me people to lead and equipped me with the Holy Spirit and His gifts to do the work. That night in Mozambique, I realized it was time to stop hyper-focusing on my calling. I'd been consumed with "worry" about it, completely missing the fact that I was already doing what He had called me to. I was already a missionary. My mission field was my home city; God had placed me in Orange County, California, among many spiritually poor people who didn't even realize their poverty and need. He'd planted me in a culture and among a people who desperately needed Him.

I had the privilege of continuing what I was already doing: earnestly seeking Him, studying, learning, pressing in for more, sharing genuinely and vulnerably with others, glorifying Him with my words and actions, using my voice for the voiceless orphans in South Africa, and inviting people around me into a deeper walk with the living God.

# Forty

## JUST DO IT

• • •

One Sunday in November, I read on social media that a pastor at my church was asking people to pray for his ten-year-old son, who had suffered from epilepsy his whole life. It was getting worse, and there were days when he had hundreds of seizures.

Remembering what had happened when I prayed for Magdalena in Mozambique, I felt prompted to reach out and ask if I could go to his house and pray for his son. I was nervous even to send the email. This was a pastor's son. I was just a regular person with no formal training; I'd never even been to seminary. What if he said no and thought I was a total weirdo?

He accepted the invitation, and one evening I drove over to his house.

I had met the pastor only a handful of times. He introduced me to his wife and son, and we chatted for a few minutes as they told me about the boy's condition, the years of struggle, the various doctors and diagnoses, the tests and procedures, their exhaustion and frustration. Removing a small vial of anointing oil from my purse, I poured some in my hand, dipped my finger into it, and made a cross on the boy's forehead. Opening my Bible, I read Psalm 91. This was a family who had faith in God and lived in His shelter; they called on Him and He was their refuge. Psalm 91 says that if these things are true, then God will give rest; He will rescue, protect, send angels to them, and reward them. I laid my hands on the boy's head and prayed, inviting the Holy Spirit to come and have His way. I rebuked Satan and told him that none of his weapons against this boy and this family would prosper. I spoke to the boy's brain, commanding it to be healed in the name of Jesus Christ.

When I was finished, I didn't feel anything. Nothing happened to suggest that the Lord had miraculously healed this child. But I knew I had done what the Lord wanted me to do. After saying good night, I went home.

The next day, I checked in with my pastor, who told me his son hadn't had any seizures since I'd been there. The following day, I checked in again and he was still seizure free. The next day, no seizures. The next week, no seizures. The next month, no seizures.

As I write this, it's been about a year and a half since I prayed for him, and he has not had a single seizure during that time.

## · WHAT IF? ·

God showed up and performed a miracle. It was like a story out of the Bible, and it was incredible for me to experience Him that way. For a long time, I'd wanted to be involved in something like that. Taking everything I had read about and learned, I put my faith in God and believed He is who He says He is, so He can do what He says He will do. I took a risk and *acted* like I believed what I said I did, which gave Him the opportunity to show up and move on that child's behalf.

I was humbled and in awe of God and His faithfulness, love, and power. I was able to help bring relief to this boy and his family and glorify God. It was amazing that He would allow me to partner with Him in this way.

What if this kind of miraculous healing became the norm because we believed the authority He's given us to use the name of Jesus? What if we stepped out in faith more often, trusted God's Word, and simply acted like everything He said is true?

More people would be healed. More would experience this kind of miracle. More would come face to face with the power of the living God—because we acted like we believed.

# Forty-One

## WHAT HIS PRESENCE CAN BE LIKE

...

I started spending extended amounts of time with the Lord early every morning. I would crawl out of bed, grab a cup of coffee, and head to the little nook I put together for God and me. It became crucial for me to have that intimate time with Him before I tackled the day's demands. Sitting in my green chair, I'd snuggle under my red blanket, take a couple of sips of my coffee, and start with, "Good morning, Lord."

This has been our special time for the last few years, and every day He meets me there. Just all at once, He comes and it begins to feel like there's a heavy blanket on top of me—it's similar to how an X-ray radiation blanket feels. The air fills with thickness and warmth; the peace is so intense I can almost hear it, and it seems like everything is happening in slow motion. He and I have real conversations, and in those moments, it's like nothing else matters.

He always teaches me something. One morning He reminded me that He's able to accomplish infinitely more through me than I can request or even think of. When I asked Him how, He answered, "Through My mighty power at work inside of you." He directed me to Ephesians 1:19–20:

*I also pray that you will understand the incredible greatness of God's power for us who believe him. This is the same mighty power that raised Christ from the dead and seated him in the place of honor at God's right hand in the heavenly realms.*

I felt Him reinforcing one thought within me over and over again: "The power that raised Christ from the dead is available to you."

Then He led me to Colossians 1:27, where it speaks of His mysterious plan of Christ living in us. He repeated, "I live in you—*in you.*" That morning, the revelation that He is actually alive inside of me took root in my heart. Because He is alive inside me, it means I have power, dominion, and authority over the powers of the unseen world. They have nothing on me, because Christ is alive in me. This means there should be no sickness or disease in my body. It means that as I walk through my home, He is literally there too. The enemy isn't welcome and doesn't have permission to be anywhere near my children. Everywhere I go, as I usher in the very presence of God, the atmosphere should change. When I touch sick and hurting people, healing should come instantly because of the power at work inside of me, the very power that raised Christ from the dead.

As followers of Jesus, we should bring peace, healing, and love to everyone, everywhere. That is His plan for my life—and for yours.

When it is time for these intimate encounters with the Lord to end, I always walk away filled up. The supernatural exchange that happens in those moments changes me little by little. I am being transformed as He renews my mind. As I die to self, which means putting aside my agenda and my way of doing things, I am resurrected to new life in Christ.

Every time I come to understand more thoroughly who I am in Christ, I feel full of His love and want to share it with others, which is one reason this book exists: so hopefully you can know His love better too.

# Forty-Two

## ASK AND RECEIVE

...

In early March 2017, I went to the Open Heavens conference at Bethel Church in Redding. I heard Kris Vallotton, one of the speakers and a pastor at Bethel, say, "When you pray for something, God will send you an example in another person of what you can become."

Like I said, I'd been praying for years that God would reveal to me, clearly and concisely, what He was calling me to. I wanted to know for sure how He desired me to use my life. Obviously, Gerda had been an incredible influence, taking on the role of my spiritual mother and raising me in the faith. She was a beautiful example of a surrendered life, and she taught me so much about the Word, caring for the poor, and what it really looks like to live out your faith. I knew that being involved with Acres of Love and orphans in South Africa was *part* of my calling. Committed to that work for the rest of my life, I would continue to plead the cause and invite others to come and join us.

But I also knew God was "expanding my territory" and preparing me for something in addition to helping Acres of Love. I knew He wanted me to write, speak, and encourage other people, and I felt He had given me the gift of healing and wanted me to begin to explore and practice it. I also sensed that I would lead a ministry of some sort and challenge believers to seek God, follow Jesus, and let Him use them. After much study, I strongly felt that all my thoughts about my calling were confirmed in Scripture.

However, just because God had shown me a *glimpse* of a future time when I would be executing my assignment didn't mean it was all about to happen right now. David was anointed as the future king of Israel when he was a young boy and didn't start reigning as king until about twenty years later. God uses times of waiting to prepare and train us up. Even though I had a sense of what God wanted to use me for, I had no idea how it would happen or when it would start.

I began to ask Him to send me another mentor, a woman, who was already doing the work He had called me to.

One day I was invited to join a study of the Holy Spirit's gifts led by my friend Blaine Cook. He had asked some of his friends and colleagues to come and teach us on specific areas they were anointed in. One of these people was his friend Marne, who shared her testimony with us. Since her childhood, she's been aware of the supernatural, and she clearly hears from the Lord.

At one point, she looked over at me, made eye contact, and out of nowhere said, "You are a soul magnet. You attract women. You will be involved in women's ministry."

It was like she looked right into my soul and knew me.

"God spoke to me about you," she said, "and I am sharing with you what I heard Him say."

Every time a stranger "reads my mail" prophetically, I feel known by God; I become aware all over again that He sees me. This time in particular was a sweet confirmation that I was on the right track and that I had, in fact, been hearing from Him myself.

Blaine then had his friend Cathy Greer spend a few weeks with us teaching more on the topic of hearing God's voice and the prophetic.

Cathy and her husband, Stuart, are the founders of Mission Support Network. They travel around the world working with indigenous apostolic leaders to advance the Kingdom of God through church planting, equipping pastors and leaders, preaching the gospel, ministering to the poor, and demonstrating the Kingdom of God in power. The stories she shared were incredible, her faith was infectious, and her knowledge of the Word inspired me. *I found myself thinking, I want to be just like her when I grow up!*

As scary as it could be, I loved her style of having us practice our spiritual gifts when we were all together. She encouraged us to take risks and said we would grow most in immediate obedience. One morning, she had us pray for Julie, who was new to the group, and told us to share anything we heard from God.

My heart started pounding, and a wave of heat came over me. I was afraid to speak up and share the impression that had come to me. What if I was totally off base and felt like an idiot for thinking I had heard from God?

Reluctantly I said, "I doubt this is anything, but when I started praying for Julie, out of nowhere, my left shoulder started hurting."

Julie gasped. "I can't believe you said that," she said and shared that she had been in a car accident two days ago and badly hurt her left shoulder.

I was just as astonished as Julie and everyone else in the room. Cathy explained to us that this was a word of knowledge. God was manifesting this pain in my shoulder to tell me what was going on in Julie. Cathy added that He often speaks this way so we will know how to pray for people.

"I believe that God wants to heal Julie," Cathy said. So she had me go over to Julie, lay my hands on her left shoulder, and pray for healing.

Afterward, Julie moved her arm up and down, rotating it around. Tears filled her eyes, and she started giggling as she reported the pain was completely gone.

The second week Cathy was teaching us, she said to me, "God told me that we're supposed to meet for coffee."

I was taken aback. God told her what? But I was excited about the opportunity to get to know her better. We exchanged phone numbers and met a few days later.

"I'm really not sure why I'm here," she said, "but God told me to meet with you. I'm wondering if maybe I'm supposed to mentor you."

I remembered my request for a female mentor who was already doing what God was calling me to. I smiled, shook my head in disbelief, and said, "Yep, you are!"

A few days later, I was studying Luke 4:18–19:

*The Spirit of the LORD is upon me,*
*for he has anointed me to bring Good News to the poor.*
*He has sent me to proclaim that captives will be released,*
*that the blind will see,*
*that the oppressed will be set free,*
*and that the time of the LORD's favor has come.*

These words, originally spoken by the prophet Isaiah and then read by Jesus in a synagogue in Nazareth, moved my heart. After Jesus read this passage aloud, He declared in verse 21, "The Scripture you've just heard has been fulfilled this very day!" If the Spirit of the Lord anointed Jesus to do these works, and I am a follower of Jesus and called into the same ministry, then I have the same anointing to do the same work. I am assigned to the poor, the captive, the blind, and the oppressed to proclaim the good news that they are healed and free forever.

"God," I prayed, "use my life. Send me wherever and to whomever You want."

And God spoke to me. His words came to me as clear as day, like I heard them aloud. He told me I would work with women who believed in Him. I would usher in the Holy Spirit so they would personally encounter Him. He didn't want just another teacher or speaker, but He wanted me to focus on His presence, which changes everything. He told me to get busy, that He would open doors and make a way for me. Interaction with Him was key; I was going to encounter and experience His real, lasting power.

That morning, He downloaded many things to me, painting a beautiful picture of how He wanted to use me to impact women and help establish His Kingdom in dark, broken places. For years, I had waited and pleaded with Him to tell me why I was here, what He wanted to do with me, and today He finally did, speaking in no uncertain terms.

Cathy and I began to meet regularly. She would encourage me, pray for me, and advise me. A short time later, I was helping her plan a women's conference, and she said, "I want you to be one of the speakers."

I gaped at her. Me? A speaker at a women's conference? This was what I'd always wanted to do—what I had visions of and what I had been praying about. God was opening doors for me, just like He said He would, and providing the opportunities I'd been praying for. He was giving me the desires of my heart.

Around the same time, after years of walking closely together and dreaming of how God was going to use us, my friend Sue and I felt it was time for us to launch our first women's discipleship group. The Lord had taken us on an amazing journey, bringing people into our lives through whom He could reveal so much to us about who He is and who we are in Him. He had shown us what it looks like to really believe Him and align our lives with our beliefs. Passionate about sharing all we had learned over the years, we wanted to invite other women into a deeper, more victorious, life-giving relationship with the Lord, with a focus on personally encountering God.

We wrote our curriculum based on our experiences, the Word, and all the other amazing resources we had discovered over the years. After spending the summer of 2017 praying, planning, studying, and writing, we started our first group, The Path, in September with fifteen women.

Also that fall, Cathy invited Sue and me to be a part of a small ministry team she was leading to India. Partnering with an organization called India Christian Ministries, she was putting on three women's conferences to empower and equip female believers from impoverished rural villages.

India had never been on my radar; my heart was really for South Africa. But I felt the Lord was providing this opportunity to travel to another nation, minister to women, and learn more from Cathy. Things were happening fast, and I saw the answers to many of my prayers. I could clearly see that God was moving. He was leading and teaching me, exposing me to new places and people, and providing a clearer vision of my future with Him.

As I watched all these things occur, I stood there in awe of what the Lord had done in my life to lead me to this point, where I was doing exactly what I wanted to do for Him: ministering to women, teaching and speaking, traveling to other parts of the world, serving the poor, praying for healing, and helping establish the Kingdom of God.

# Forty-Three

## IN THE WAITING

• • •

Mark and I were on a date night, sitting at the bar of our favorite restaurant in town. I excitedly told him about all the opportunities that were coming up for me and asked for his blessing to travel to India in the fall. I honestly thought I would get it.

To my surprise, Mark did not share my excitement about all these new and time-consuming endeavors. "I'm concerned about how much time you're spending away from us," he said. "You're preoccupied with other things. I wish you would consider going back to work and reshifting your focus and energy back to our home and our family. Honestly, with every new commitment you take on, it's hard for me." He let me know that he was growing more and more resentful.

I learned that evening that he'd been feeling increasingly concerned about how much I had changed over the recent years. While he was always supportive of my journey and happy I had found the Lord, he was upset that I was no longer anything like the woman he had married fifteen years prior. From his perspective, I had lost balance in my life because I was dedicating so much of my time to studying the Bible, traveling, and going to prayer meetings and conferences. He felt hurt, like I had left him behind and chosen God as a priority over him and the kids.

I stared at him in shock. It was like I had gotten the wind knocked out of me. Just when things were beginning to pick up speed and it seemed that God was making all my dreams come true, Mark wanted everything to slow down. What was I supposed to do now? It seemed obvious to me that God was at work in my life. He had brought Cathy to me and provided me with all these new ministry opportunities that were totally in line with everything I had been praying for. How was I going to follow Him and be used by Him when my husband wanted more of my time, energy, and focus?

At first I was angry with Mark, but as I cooled down, I began to feel sad too. I regretted that I had made him feel this way. It was never my intention for him or the kids to feel like I was "preoccupied" with the Lord. I was following Him in part because I believed it was the best thing I could do for my family—this was *for* them, in a way. So what had gone wrong?

Waiting means staying where you are or delaying action until a particular time or until something else happens. Beginning that evening, I found myself in a painful place of waiting. There was nothing I could do in this situation but wait for something to shift. I had to trust God in new ways—not in the going and doing but in the very slow process of every day and hoping He would change my husband's heart. I had to trust the vision He had given me for my life, trust that He had put Mark and me together, and trust that He was at work in the midst of everything that was going on. Waiting has never been easy for me. It is hard to feel powerless, knowing I am fully unable to make something happen.

That season was marked by tears, desperation, and prayer. Mark, I realized, had never had a powerful revelation of who God is. In a manner of speaking, he was still waiting for his radical, life-transforming encounter with the Lord. When I became aware of this, I wanted God to do something—to show up and reveal Himself. I knew that Mark was just one encounter away from knowing God the way I did and surrendering his life to the Lord's plan for him. And for all of us.

I began to pray fervently for Mark every day, asking God to break through and crash in on him. Though it was true that he and I weren't quite as close as we used to be, it seemed to me that my husband's negative feelings about my commitment to the Lord weren't entirely *his* feelings; it seemed more likely they were the enemy's schemes against God's plans. So I took authority over my marriage, my family, and my home, and I canceled any assignment the devil had against us. I clung to Scriptures that promised a new heart for my husband, a heart that was tender and responsive (Ezek. 36:26). I reminded the Lord that He promised wonderful results for earnest prayers (James 5:16) and that I was assured He heard my requests and would give me what I asked for (1 John 5:14–15).

Even though my hopes appeared to be at a standstill in the natural, especially where India was concerned, I determined not to look at the situation with my human eyes. I took God at His Word and believed what He said, not placing any weight on my frustrations and fears.

During this season of contending for Mark's relationship with the Lord and spiritual unity for us, I felt like God told me, "No striving! Defer to Mark." I knew He was telling me to recommit to Mark, to humble myself and respect my husband, waiting on God until He sovereignly intervened.

I did my best. I talked with Mark at length about what he wanted from me and how he wanted things to be different in our marriage, with our kids, and in our home. I made genuine efforts to connect with him and show him he was a priority in my life. I worked on discipline and consistency with the kids, put myself on a budget, and tried to limit my spending. I shifted more of my focus, time, and energy back into my home and family. Our marriage began to thrive again, and both Mark and I relished the newfound intimacy we were sharing.

All the while, God was encouraging me and building me up. He was faithful to remind me of who He is and that He was still moving in my life. One day I had three amazing encounters that helped bring me peace. The first occurred at the spiritual-gifts study with Blaine Cook. A young missionary girl, someone I had never met, came over to me and said, "The Lord tells me that you're a leader. You're a voice for the orphan. You're going to call out women and tell them there's more. You're going to wake up the church."

Considering what was happening in my life right then and everything that seemed up in the air, her words really spoke to me.

A couple of hours later, I received a random text from Cathy. "Everything God has promised you is a Yes and Amen!" she wrote. Again, I felt the weight of those words and knew God was speaking to me.

That afternoon at the spa, I had a massage from a therapist from India. While she was working on me, God gave me clear insight into her personality and her struggles, and I saw a vision of a painful situation involving her oldest son. I saw her entire family in their kitchen, and her husband was cutting their son's long hair. The boy was so angry and she was crying. I began to get a sharp pain in my head.

"Do you get headaches?" I asked her.

She paused, looking at me in surprise. "I get terrible migraines."

As I shared with her what the Lord was showing me about her and her family, she started weeping. She told me that they were of the Sikh faith. The men wear turbans and don't cut their hair. After 9/11, the men in her family began to experience horrible persecution because of the way they looked. She and her husband required their sons to keep their hair long and wear their turbans, even though they were being treated terribly at school. Finally, when it became too difficult to handle, they cut their sons' hair. The oldest boy was furious that they had made him wait so long and suffer so much, and their relationship became strained. She was devastated and heartbroken over this strife in her family.

After the massage, I asked if I could pray for her and she agreed. I prayed for her headaches and for healing in her family. When I sensed the Lord prompt me, I asked, "Do you know Jesus?"

"I know who He is," she replied, "but I don't know Him personally. I have been praying that God would send someone to talk to me about Him."

I shared the gospel with her and told her how much God loved her because He had sent me that day to invite her into a relationship with Him. She accepted His invitation, and we hugged and cried together.

These three encounters, all in one day, increased my faith and reminded me that God was with me. Even though I was frustrated and confused about how everything was going to work out, I knew that God was moving in the situation. He graciously tended to me.

A few days later in a prayer meeting at Blaine Cook's house, the Lord spoke to me during worship. He lovingly reminded me that His Spirit is inside of me, and He told me to declare victory. He had already conquered sin and death, and the work was finished; I was more than a conqueror because I am His and He is mine. He told me to use the name of Jesus, that it contained all power and authority. I needed to claim it and speak it over Mark, my marriage, my children, and every dark place where the enemy is—over disease, every stronghold, every sin, lie, addiction, chain, and shackle. He told me to stop waiting and instead go and do. I could declare victory and have victory.

"Resistance has lifted," He said. "There is openness ahead."

# • WHAT IF? •

According to the Word of God, because I was a follower of Christ, I had all authority and power to use the name of Jesus Christ of Nazareth to cast out demons and heal the sick. For years, I thought I believed this—but did I really? Because if I did, why wasn't I spending more time and effort doing those things? It must be that I didn't really believe. I didn't really have faith for it.

In the book of John, Jesus was very good friends with three siblings: Mary, Martha, and Lazarus. While Jesus was away in Jerusalem around the time of Hanukkah, Lazarus became very sick and his sisters sent word to Jesus. Two days later, Jesus made His way to Bethany to see them, but Lazarus had died and they'd already buried him. Mary and Martha were overcome with grief, and Jesus Himself was deeply troubled and wept with them.

"Your brother will rise again," Jesus said. "Where have you put him?"

When they arrived at the tomb, Jesus instructed, "Roll the stone aside."

"Oh, but, Lord," Martha protested. "He has been dead for four days. The smell will be terrible."

Martha knew who Jesus was. She called him Lord and to His face told Him she had always believed He was the Messiah, the Son of God. Yet when Jesus told her that Lazarus would rise again, she was faced with this question: "Do I really believe what I claim to believe?"

Jesus said to her, "Didn't I tell you that you would see God's glory if you believe?"

That word *if* is of monumental importance. We will see God's glory, His power and majesty—*if* we believe. So if we don't believe, if we lack faith, shrink back, or doubt, we will miss out on seeing who He really is and what He can really do.

Faith requires commitment and boldness. It requires risk and puts us at a crossroads every time: What do we believe? In order to encounter God and experience Him, we have to do our part. We have to make the first move and exhibit faith. Then as we do, He will meet us and display His glory.

In this season of waiting on the Lord to move in my life, I had to trust His instructions to me. I needed to yield, defer, and have faith, believing that even though I couldn't see things changing in the physical realm, He was working. *If* I believed Him, I would see His glory.

# *Forty-Four*

## THE RESPONSE TO TRUST

...

I hadn't spoken to Mark about India for months. It seemed like it was a lost cause, like there was no way I was going to get his blessing for that trip. But things were better between us and more cohesive at home. It had proven to be a good season for us as we focused on our marriage and family.

Early one Saturday morning, I climbed out of bed and did my quiet time. Then I showered and got dressed and made a nice breakfast. When Mark came downstairs, I handed him a cup of coffee and invited him to sit at the kitchen table with me. I told him there was a commitment meeting later that morning for any of the women who were going to India.

"Could I go?" I asked.

He took a deep breath and said, "The only reason I am even considering this is because things have been so great around here lately. Go ahead to the meeting."

In Matthew 19:26, Jesus says, "Humanly speaking, it is impossible. But with God everything is possible." If I had relied on my circumstances only, I would have given up. I would have thought it was all over, that my dreams of ministry were unattainable, and with great disappointment I would have settled. But God's Word, which is truth, told me something different. It told me that I could trust Him, that He was with me, that He had a good plan for me, that I was called to the work of the ministry of Jesus Christ, that I was filled with the power of the Holy Spirit, and that He wanted to use my life to accomplish His purposes. When I was confused and alarmed, I clung to those promises. I reviewed them daily, reminded God of them, wrote about them in my journal, prayed like they were true, and expected God to move in a powerful way. And He did—I was going to India!

Cathy called me later that week to say she wanted me to be one of the speakers at the three conferences we would be putting on in India. For about two hours at each conference, I would be speaking on the topic of healing.

Of course—healing! As honored and excited as I was, I also felt terribly nervous because I was my no means an expert on the topic. I had only just begun pressing into the gift; I was still learning about it myself and had experienced only a few instances of breakthrough. Was I really equipped to teach on it?

That afternoon as I was doing dishes and thinking about the trip to India, I considered how I would approach my teaching. I was standing at the kitchen sink, and God spoke to me. He said, "When you teach in India, healing will break out among the women. I want you to use that story as the end of your book."

## • WHAT IF? •

As always, faith set me at a crossroads. I could choose to respond in fear—because this was new and I hadn't ever done this before—or I could choose to really believe everything Jesus was teaching me.

Why are so many of us afraid to take risks and act like we believe? Perhaps we're afraid of what other people will think of us. Fear of man is such an easy trap to fall into, and Satan uses it all the time to paralyze us. Or perhaps we aren't seeing the true power of God because we don't really believe Him for it. We stop short in our faith, or we don't fully believe what Scripture says. If we don't believe Him, it means we don't trust that He is who He says He is and can do what He says He can do. We're basically calling Him a liar, which must grieve His heart. We play a huge part in His ability to be seen at work. He won't force us to do what He says; He's a gentleman. So in order to experience Him, we have to do our part.

Doing our part looks like faith. We have to act in faith, get in motion, and take the next step. The giants of our faith, the men and women we look up to because they inspire us, acted like they believed. They went for it, taking God at His Word and making decisions based on what they believed to be the truth. When I see people who are surrounded by God—by His works, His words, His people, His life—but they remain unmoved by Him, it seems evident to me that they haven't actually experienced Him. When we don't respond in faith, we show with our actions what we believe.

If we believe and act like it, we will see Him and truly know Him. Many who fill our churches today know a great deal about Christ, but they don't know Him personally. They don't combine their knowledge with faith. When we trust in Christ, we do what He says. We become *believing believers.*

# forty-five

## BLIND EYES

...

I was in India. This country was never on my radar. Honestly, I'd never even thought about it. But God wasn't surprised. He had led me there through a wild twelve-year journey with Him. Now I was sitting on a stage in front of hundreds of Indian women preparing to teach them on healing. It seemed like so many things were all coming together in that moment, and God was showing me more of who He is and what He is capable of.

Some of the dresses in the audience were gorgeous with beautiful fabric and gold stitching. Some were old and tattered with holes, the colors faded. I was wearing a traditional Indian outfit as well, which they loved. Barefoot, tired, and dirty, they were weighed down with all sorts of burdens, physical ailments, and diseases. Many of them had traveled long distances to attend the conference. They were poor women, most of them fieldworkers and uneducated. They had never been to something like this before, where they could sit with other Christian women and be the focus of our teaching, encouragement, and attention. They were used to being outcast, disrespected, overlooked.

Looking out over the crowd, I was keenly aware of the country's lack of religious freedom. Most people in India are Muslim or Hindu. On our way to the conference that day, we had driven right through the middle of a protest by a radical Muslim group. The pastor who was putting on the conference had been threatened for his faith, and there was a price on his head. The reality of everyday life for the Christian women in this country was at the forefront of my mind. I couldn't possibly understand what they went through, what their lives were like, and the persecution they faced.

As I stood center stage, microphone in hand, I battled feelings of doubt. Who was I to teach them? I was just an ordinary person, a wife and stay-at-home mom from blessed Orange County, California. I had been walking with the Lord for only twelve years and didn't have any formal training; I certainly wasn't a pastor. I was there only because of God's leading. The only way I was qualified to be there on that stage was because He had qualified me.

Early this morning, I had asked God to reveal to me a physical condition He wanted to heal in the women who would be at the conference. I felt like He told me He wanted to heal women of tooth, chest, and back pain. So at the end of my teaching time, I said, "Those of you who are suffering from these things, stand up."

I invited the Holy Spirit to come and heal them. I rebuked the enemy and commanded the pain to leave their bodies, using the name of Jesus Christ.

"If you were healed," I said, "wave your hands in the air so we can all see and give thanks to God."

My heart racing, I stood there and watched as multiple hands shot into the air, testifying of healing. We invited a few of the women who were healed to come forward and share what had happened to them.

"When I came to the conference this morning," one woman said into the microphone, "my chest was hurting terribly. I was very short of breath and could only walk a few steps before I would feel exhausted and winded. God healed me while you prayed, and now I am singing and dancing, worshipping with so much joy."

Another woman said she had suffered for three years with neck and back pain, and now she was totally pain free. Another shared that she'd had pain in her right arm and shoulder, so much that she couldn't lift her arm; she had to keep it down by her side. Laughing excitedly, she announced that God had completely healed her and showed us how she could lift her arm up over her head.

One woman told us she'd been in pain for weeks because of stones in both kidneys. She couldn't even sit in a chair at the conference but had been lying on the floor at the back of the room. "While you were praying," she said, "I felt heat all over my body and then the pain instantly disappeared." She got up off the floor and was completely healed.

At the end of the conference's first day, a woman rushed up on the stage as we were getting ready to leave. Panicked, she was crying hysterically and holding a baby girl who had a high fever. The child was lethargic and lay there lifelessly on the mother's chest. We couldn't understand what she was saying, but we could sense the urgency. As a team, we laid our hands on the baby and prayed for healing.

The next day, the woman returned and shared with everyone that the little girl had typhoid fever, and a doctor had said days earlier that she needed to be admitted to the hospital immediately. "I didn't have money to take the baby to the hospital," the woman told us, "so I asked God to heal her." She brought the baby to the conference yesterday so we could pray for her, and last night the baby slept well for the first time in weeks. The fever was completely gone, and the baby was alert, had color in her cheeks, and was full of energy.

The room broke out in praise. All the women celebrated and lifted their hands and voices to the Lord. Our team was ecstatic; all of this was such a blessing.

A few days later, we flew to a different city to hold the second conference. On Sunday we drove out to a little village to dedicate a small church, and after the dedication, right before we left the village, we were invited to drive out several more miles to another remote village to pray for some land, where the ministry was hoping to build another church. We took long, bumpy, dusty dirt roads to get there. As we pulled up to the land, we saw the woman from the first conference standing in the road holding her baby. We all shouted and jumped out of the car, yelling in amazement, "It's the lady with the baby!"

We greeted her with hugs and kisses. She couldn't believe we were there, and we were astonished that she lived in the village we had randomly decided to visit. Everyone in her village had heard about the miracle of the baby's healing and graciously welcomed us. We learned this woman had taken the baby girl on a ten-hour bus ride to attend the conference and have us pray. God blessed us so much by letting us see her and her baby again.

As I was preparing to teach at the second conference, I woke up early to pray, and I asked God what I had asked Him the last time: to tell me the conditions He wanted to heal that day. It was four o'clock in the morning, and I was lying in the dark under the covers. I felt God telling me that He wanted to heal blind eyes.

"No, God," I argued. "Not blind eyes. That's too big! Can't we do something smaller, something easier? Please give me something else." I instantly felt a pain in the ball of my right foot. "Okay, great—let's go with pain in the right foot. That's easier."

My phone buzzed, lighting up on the nightstand next to me. It was a text from my friend Gretchen, who was back home in the United States:

*Word for you today . . . eyes will be opened! I was on a run, listening to the song "Holy Spirit Come," thinking about those women in the picture you sent me yesterday. Praying for you guys and your message today. I heard God saying, "Eyes will be opened."*

Well, there was no denying it now. Gretchen's text confirmed that God wanted to heal blind eyes that day.

Should I go for it? This kind of healing felt radical to me, and my stomach rolled at the thought of standing in front of a large group of women and declaring that God was going to heal this way. What if I prayed for blind women, and they *weren't* healed? How embarrassing would that be?

But in order for me to encounter God, experience Him, and really see His power, I knew I had to take this risk. It would require me to step out, which was exactly what I was telling the women at the conference to do as I taught them about healing.

During worship at the beginning of the conference, I got down on my knees and put my face to the floor. In tears, I asked God to show up and come in power, to open the floodgates and let rivers of living water flow through me. I pleaded with Him to flood that room and let the women be consumed in His loving presence. I was very aware that there was nothing I could really do apart from Him. He had to show up.

As I lay on the floor, I felt warmth come over my body and a sense of heaviness that had become familiar to me over the years. It was like waves and waves of His presence were flowing over me, and I knew the Lord was right there with me.

As one of the other team members spoke, Sue tapped my arm and pointed to something she'd written in her journal: "And it is impossible to please God without faith" (Heb. 11:6).

Again, the challenge was presented to me. Would I take this risk that, in my head, still seemed very hard? In order to please God, I needed to obey Him. And in order to obey Him in this situation, I needed to display my faith. He would show up here today—if I acted like I believed.

Later as I finished up my lesson, butterflies filled my stomach. "I believe God wants to heal blind eyes today," I said and invited every woman with blindness to stand and receive prayer.

About ten women stood up. Taking a deep, steadying breath, I welcomed the Holy Spirit and asked Him to come and bring healing to these women. In the name of Jesus Christ of Nazareth, I spoke to their bodies and told them to be healed, and I commanded all blindness to leave. I rebuked Satan, reminding him that he was a defeated foe, and I canceled any assignment against these women.

As I was praying, something happened. I realized I had raised my right hand and stretched it out over the crowd. I wasn't praying calmly anymore. I was yelling into the microphone. It felt like something had taken over my body and was speaking for me. I could hear myself—but couldn't believe it was me. What was this? I wasn't thinking about what I was saying or what I looked like or sounded like. Faith burned within me, and the room filled with energy until the whole place began to feel electric and alive. I told the women to believe for their healing, receive it, and thank God for it.

"Any of you who were healed of any blindness, wave your hands high above your head so we can all see," I said.

Six women excitedly waved their hands, and the room exploded with shouts and cheers of praise. On the stage we all jumped up and down, clapped, and celebrated. This was like nothing any of us had ever experienced, and emotion overwhelmed us. A couple of the women who were healed came forward to share their testimonies on the microphone, and our translator, fighting back her own emotions, told us what they were saying:

"She had a sight problem. She was not able to read small letters. And when she prayed, she is able to see now. She can read the letters in the Bible.

"She had an eye problem. She was only able to see with her right eye, not her left one. Now the darkness has gone, and she is able to see with both eyes."

"She was not able to see letters. Now she is able to read the Bible."

"She was not able to identify people. She is an old lady, but now she is able to identify people and is able to see very bright things."

I collapsed in my seat and wept. It happened—God showed up. He performed miracles in our midst, and He used me to do it.

Cathy wrapped her arms around me and cried with me. She said, "You're so brave. You have so much courage. This is just the beginning. What doors He opens, no man will shut!"

Beth Moore says, "There is no high like the Most High." That day, I understood those words at a much deeper level. That was the most fun I'd ever had in my life.

# Forty-Six

## THE EDGE

...

Here we arrive at the crossroads.

We can't simply wait for God to show up and do something big in our lives. If we want to see miracles and have a personal encounter with the Lord, we have to walk out beyond the shoreline and head straight into the waves. We have to step out on the edge of the highest cliff, our toes dangling off the side, risk tingling through our veins. We have to face our fears and be brave, trusting Him to show up and do something. Offering ourselves to Him, we provide the opportunity—the platform—for Him to work.

It is time for us to believe Him and really act like it. That day in India, I had a fresh revelation of the Scripture Sue pointed out to me before I walked up on stage: "It is impossible to please God without faith" (Heb. 11:6).

Take the risk. Go for it.

God showed up in India. His presence came into that room filled with women who were poor, many of them tired and in pain. He healed blind eyes right there in front of me—while I prayed for them.

It was the most ridiculous, radical, unbelievable thing. *Finally.* Finally I got to see, with my own eyes, what I had only heard and read about.

God is real. He is everything He says He is in His Word. It's all true. He's intimately involved in our lives. He is for us and in us, and He has equipped us. He wants to use us. He created us, knows us, loves us, and speaks to us. He leads us. And He performs miracles.

That trip summed up everything I believed God had told me about my calling, the things He'd promised me and put on my heart. Every Scripture I had read, every sermon I had heard, every book I studied, every worship song I poured my heart into, every prophetic word I received, every prayer I prayed, every morning I had gotten up long before my family to spend precious time with my heavenly Father, every journal entry I wrote, every vision I had of my future, every word I heard my Lord whisper in my ear—it was all for that moment. But not just for that moment. This was just the beginning. This was my starting point.

That night on our long drive back to the hotel, I wanted to be alone with God, in the dark. I sat in the back of the car, put my ear buds in so no one would talk to me, cranked up my worship music, and wrote in my journal.

I had discovered the answer to my heart's question. I had so badly wanted to know, "What if?" What if I really believed God and then acted like it? I had wondered what would happen, had dreamed about what it would look like, hoping that someday I would truly experience, for myself, God's power and might and majesty. And I had. Choosing to take Him at His Word, I stepped into faith on that stage in India. I believed Him—I *really* believed Him—and acted like it. And the result was that I was able to encounter Him in a way I never had.

God is everything the Bible says He is.

He is real. He is powerful. He is faithful.

Today, He waits to encounter you.

# BIBLIOGRAPHY

...

Baker, Heidi. *Compelled by Love: How to Change the World Through the Simple Power of Love in Action.* Lake Mary, FL: Charisma House, 2013.

Chambers, Oswald. *My Utmost for His Highest.* Grand Rapids, MI: Discovery House, 1992.

Clark, Randy. *There Is More! The Secret to Experiencing God's Power to Change Your Life.* Ada, MI: Chosen Books, 2013.

Conwell, Russell. *Acres of Diamonds.* Philadelphia: John Y. Huber Company, 1890.

Stearns, Richard. *The Hole in Our Gospel: What Does God Expect of Us?* Nashville: Thomas Nelson, 2009.

# LEARN MORE

• • •

For more information about supporting
Acres of Love,
*please visit*
www.acresoflove.org

• • •